Excel

PRIMARY SPELLING HANDBOOK

Phil Walker

Reprinted 2008, 2015, 2016, 2017 (twice), 2020 (twice), 2022, 2023

ISBN 978 1 74125 263 7

Pascal Press
PO Box 250
Glebe NSW 2037
(02) 9198 1748
www.pascalpress.com.au

Publisher: Vivienne Joannou
Project editor: Mark Dixon
Edited by Christine Eslick
Typeset by Ij Design (Julianne Billington)
Illustrations by Jan D'Silva (Moving Ideas Animation) and David Dickson
Cover by DiZign Pty Ltd
Printed by Vivar Printing/Green Giant Press

Contents

Contents

Contents

Introduction

The ***Excel*** **Primary Spelling Handbook** is a follow-up to the very successful *Pascal Basic Primary Spelling*.

The layout and structure will prove valuable to the following groups of students:

- **students** requiring a more comprehensive coverage of spelling and word skills
- **students from a non-English speaking background** who will benefit from a structured page-by-page approach to the development of standard English spelling.

The main objectives are:

- to review the basic sounds: vowels, consonants and blends
- to develop the ability to build words using a variety of word-building strategies (e.g. visual patterns, word families, letter clusters)
- to explore homonyms, homographs, synonyms and antonyms, and to develop dictionary skills
- to explore significant spelling rules and identify common exceptions to these rules
- to further develop word-building skills using common prefixes and suffixes
- to explore and recognise the origin of many words by studying common Latin and Greek words.

Chapters 1–6 will provide students with a greater understanding of correct spelling and increase their vocabulary development and associated word skills.

The reference section provides word lists to further develop knowledge of English spelling.

Each chapter contains the following tests:

Quick check	These are short tests at the bottom of some pages.
How much do you know?	These are one-page tests at the end of each section within a chapter.
Review tests	These are two-page tests covering the work of a complete chapter.

Answers and explanations (where necessary) have been included for self-assessment.

1 Basic sounds: vowels and consonants

In this chapter, you will practise recognising **long** and **short vowel sounds**, **consonant sounds**, and **combinations** and **blends** of letters.

Vowel sounds *a*

In this section, you will practise the **short** and **long vowel sound *a***.

Short vowel sound *a*	Long vowel sound *a*		
c**a**t	c**a**k**e**	r**ai**n	p**ay**
b**a**t	**ei**ght	th**ey**	

1 **Circle** the words that have a **short *a*** sound.

back	camp	glad	gram	pray
stand	main	thank	that	hard

2 **Circle** the words that have a **long *a*** sound.

eighteen	calf	bait	plain	today
brain	stay	glad	laughter	plate

3 **Add** the ***a*** sound to these words. Mark **S** (short) or **L** (long) in the box to describe the sound.

sp______ce	☐	displ______y	☐	gr______ze	☐
______pple	☐	br______ve	☐	bec______me	☐
t______ken	☐	spr______y	☐	sh______dy	☐

4 **Underline** the ***a*** sound in each word. Mark **S** or **L** in the box to describe the sound.

lazy	☐	train	☐	game	☐
take	☐	arrow	☐	navy	☐
swayed	☐	named	☐	among	☐

5 **Write** words in the columns below to **match** the **short** or **long sounds**.

b**a**t	c**a**k**e**	r**ai**n	p**ay**
______	______	______	______
______	______	______	______
______	______	______	______
______	______	______	______

☞ Answers on page 120

Vowel sounds e

- **Say** the word. ● **Listen** for the ***e*** sound. ● **Complete** the activities below.

Short vowel sound e	Long vowel sound e			
n**e**st	m**e**	tr**ee**	**ea**t	ch**ie**f
br**ea**d	s**ei**ze	k**ey**	bab**y**	

1 **Circle** the words that have a **short *e*** sound.

help	seven	tread	jetty	fresh
chest	peel	slept	setting	meat

2 **Circle** the words that have a **long *e*** sound.

lady	three	seat	monkey	object
relief	beetle	carry	unless	greeting

3 **Use** the letters in the long box with those in the circle to **build words** with the **short *e*** sound.

w b t r v z — est

____

____

4 **Use** the letters in the long box with those in the circle to **build words** with the **long *e*** sound.

d f h n s bl fr st — eed

____

____

5 **Underline** the **e** sound in each word. Mark **S** (short) or **L** (long) in the box to describe the sound.

screen ☐	press ☐	grief ☐
donkey ☐	leave ☐	needle ☐
nearly ☐	field ☐	ready ☐

6 **Write** words in the columns below to **match** the **short** or **long sounds**.

eat	bab**y**	ch**ie**f	fr**ee**
________	________	________	________
________	________	________	________
________	________	________	________
________	________	________	________

Answers on page 120

Vowel sounds *i*

- **Say** the words. ● **Listen** for the ***i*** sounds. ● **Complete** the activities below.

Short vowel sound *i*	Long vowel sound *i*
b**u**i**l**der, p**i**g, capt**ai**n	b**i**nd, p**ie**, cr**y**, l**igh**t, **i**ron

1 **Circle** the words that have a **short *i*** sound.

gift	knife	still	quite	spring
little	winter	silver	middle	bright

2 **Circle** the words that have a **long *i*** sound.

ticket	shine	strike	while	winner
flies	tried	sty	sighted	frighten

3 **Add** the ***i*** sound to these words. Mark **S** (short) or **L** (long) in the box to describe the sound.

dec______de ☐	sm______le ☐	s______ght ☐
ins______de ☐	tr______ed ☐	w______nner ☐
sh______ne ☐	fr______ghten ☐	sl______ck ☐

4 Make **rhyming words** for these.

pie ________________________________

cry ________________________________

light ________________________________

still ________________________________

5 **Select** a suitable word from the box to **complete each sentence**. Mark **S** or **L** in the box to describe the ***i*** sound.

fifth	sight	strike	ivory	admire
knife	reply	sly	inside	tide

a The lightning will ____________________ ☐ the barn near the paddocks.

b The small ____________________ ☐ carving was neatly done.

c The tourists will ____________________ ☐ the beauty of the island.

d She was the ____________________ ☐ in line.

e The caravan came in ____________________ ☐ a few minutes ago.

f When asked the question, the boy did not ____________________ ☐.

☞ Answers on page 120

Vowel sounds o

● **Say** the words. ● **Listen** for the ***o*** sounds. ● **Complete** the activities below.

Short vowel sound *o*	Long vowel sound *o*		
d**o**g	r**o**p**e**	c**oa**t	h**oe**
w**a**tch	cr**ow**	g**o**ld	pian**o**

1 **Circle** the words that have a **short *o*** sound.

dingo ponds logger cot yellow
shown washed locks wanted mopping

2 **Circle** the words that have a **long *o*** sound.

below coast float shallow spot
hotel blot follow toast coach

3 **Use** the letters in the long box with those in the circle to **build words** with the **long *o*** sound.

a b l s t bl fl gr sl sn — ow

____

____

b b g m gl fl bl thr — oat

____

____

4 **Add** a **short** or **long *o*** sound to complete these words. Mark **S** (short) or **L** (long) in the box to describe the sound.

shad_____	☐	p_____lite	☐	_____bey	☐
radi_____	☐	tomat_____	☐	_____cean	☐
s_____ldier	☐	t_____	☐	str_____ke	☐

5 Build new words by **changing** the **bold** letters to **short** or **long *o*** sounds. Mark **S** or **L** in the box to describe the sound.

sl**ew**	__________	☐	r**i**de	__________	☐
even	__________	☐	t**ear**	__________	☐
yell**ed**	__________	☐	dr**i**ve	__________	☐

☞ Answers on page 120

Vowel sounds *u*

- **Say** the words. ● **Listen** for the ***u*** sounds. ● **Complete** the activities below.

Short vowel sound *u*	Long vowel sound *u*
t**o**ngue, c**u**p, c**ou**ple	fl**u**te, m**oo**n, fl**ew**, gl**ue**, fr**ui**t, s**ou**p, t**u**be, stat**ue**

1 **Circle** the words that have a **short *u*** sound.

such summer bunch spoon trunk
uncle sunny few hunter number

2 **Circle** the words that have a **long *u*** sound.

grew soon shoot rude stoop
emu double suited music stew

3 **Use** the letters in the long box with those in the circle to **build words** with the **long *u*** sound.

a f h n p bl cr sl st — ew

____

____

b b n s cr sp — oon

____

____

4 **Add** the ***u*** sound to **complete these words**. Mark **S** (short) or **L** (long) in the box to describe the sound.

l_____te ☐	cr_____ner ☐	h_____ge ☐
s_____pper ☐	d_____ble ☐	n_____t ☐
zeb_____ ☐	overd_____ ☐	en_____gh ☐

5 **Select** a suitable word from the box to **complete each sentence**. Mark **S** or **L** in the box to describe the sound.

sooner true thunder supply amuse

a The work was done ______________________ ☐ than expected.

b Did the people ______________________ ☐ the goods to the shops?

c They heard the rumble of ______________________ ☐ in the distance.

☞ Answers on page 120

Vowel sounds

1 **Shade** the words with a **short vowel** sound in this word wall.

batch	crash	spread	clog	west
black	folded	awful	finger	check
lee	bullet	float	cake	stir
lighter	pays	push	strong	dance
jetty	tread	sob	stain	crazy

2 **Add** a **short** or a **long** vowel sound ***a*** to these words. **Identify** them as short or long vowel sounds by marking **S** or **L** in the box.

m______pping ☐ h______nded ☐ c______ravan ☐
m______nager ☐ pl______te ☐ str______ght ☐
r______lway ☐ p______ddock ☐

3 **Add** a **short** or **long** vowel sound ***e*** to these words. **Identify** them as short or long vowel sounds by marking **S** or **L** in the box.

sw______ting ☐ d______dly ☐ ______qual ☐
sch______me ☐ th______re's ☐ ______ither ☐
p______ceful ☐ t______nnis ☐

4 **Circle** the words with a **long *i*** vowel sound and **underline** those with a **short *i*** vowel sound.

hilltop fishy seaside knife

arrive until quite middle

family fifth

5 **Add** a **short** or **long** vowel sound ***o*** and an **ending** to these words.

st______ck_________ narr______w_________ dr______p_________
c______ch_________ sorr______ _________ sp______k_________

6 **Add** a **short** or **long** vowel sound ***u*** to these words. Identify them as short or long vowel sounds by marking **S** or **L** in the box.

d______ckling ☐ c______ple ☐ y______ng ☐
c______shion ☐ parach______te ☐ m______ddle ☐
circ______s ☐ tr______thful ☐

☞ Answers on page 120

Single consonant sounds

● **Say** the words. ● **Listen** for the sounds. ● **Complete** the activities.

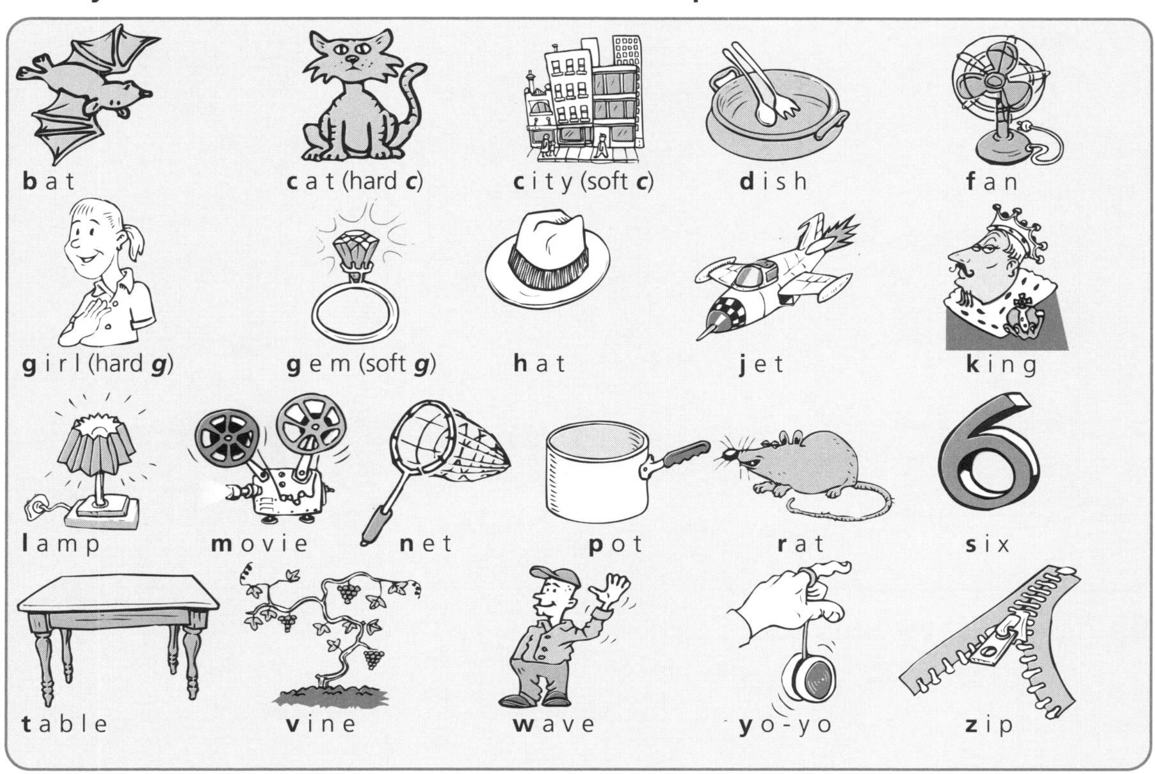

1 **Circle** the words with the **hard *c*** sound. **Underline** the words with the **soft *c*** sound.

calves	costume	century	canoe	coins
camp	canyon	cement	coconut	cavern
copper	cashew	cereal	cedar	cigar

2 **Circle** the words with the **hard *g*** sound. **Underline** the words with the **soft *g*** sound.

games	giggle	garbage	giddy	gentle
gender	girth	gases	gallop	galaxy
gauze	garden	general	gargle	germs

3 **Add** suitable **consonants** to complete these words.

________atapult	________itizen	________istant	________unnier
________azebo	________angle	________attery	________asual
________ispose	________otton	________oking	________adget
________idding	________ighter	________isery	________othing
________ossible	________ifle	________atin	________otally
________isitor	________aken	________ebra	________odel

☞ Answers on page 120

Combination sounds

● **Say** the words. ● **Listen** for the sounds. ● **Complete** the activities.

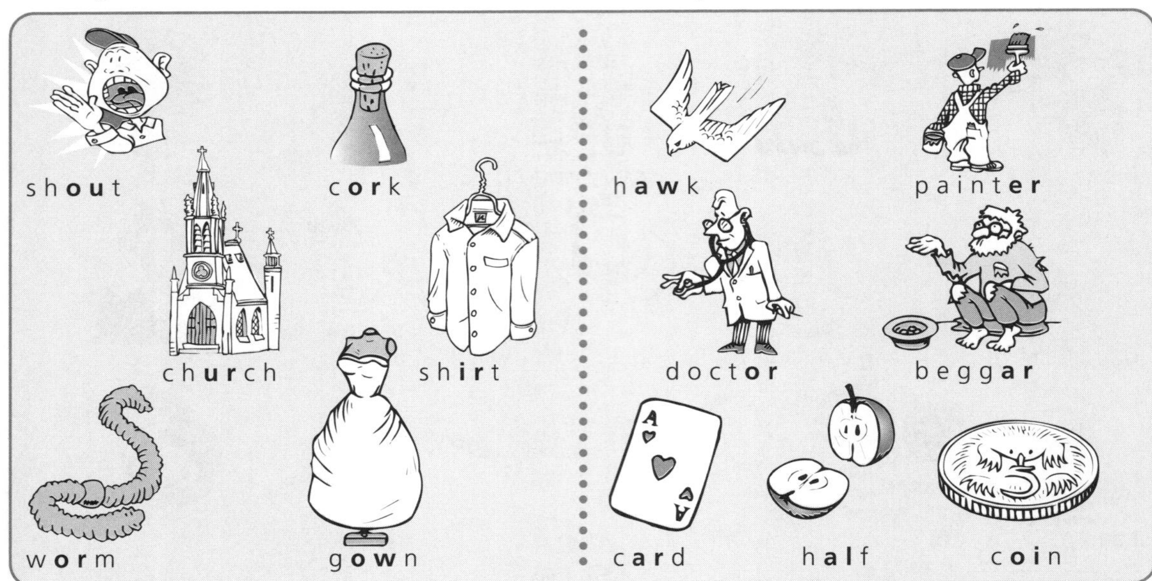

1 **Circle** the **combination sounds** shown in the box above in these words.

laughter	surveyor	fork	drawn	porch
hard	teacher	loiter	crowd	hound
liar	about	lurching		

2 **Complete** the **words** with the **sound combinations** at the end of the sentences.

- **a** The predator will p_______nce on the much smaller animal. (ou)
- **b** They will rec_______d the results on the computer. (or)
- **c** She tried not to dist_______b her sister at work. (ur)
- **d** The fluid will squ_______t from the small hole. (ir)
- **e** It was the w_______st accident for many years. (or)
- **f** Will you all_______ him to attend the concert. (ow)
- **g** The str_______ was placed in the stables. (aw)
- **h** The vehicle was put up on the h_______st. (oi)
- **i** The messeng_______ will carry the small parcel. (er)

3 **Add combination sounds** to complete these words.

s_______nd	st_______m	b_______nt	f_______st
w_______ld	b_______th	b_______st	gr_______nd
w_______st	d_______ty	n_______se	spr_______t
t_______n	cr_______l	p_______nt	st_______t
sail_______	beginn_______	p_______ty	h_______dship
m_______ch	h_______st		

Answers on page 121

Initial blends

● **Say** the words. ● **Listen** for the blends. ● **Complete** the activities.

1 **Complete** the phrases using words built with the **initial blends** indicated in **bold**.

- a **bl**________ of grass
- b handle of the **br**________
- c **cl**________ the mountain
- d **cr**________ of the hill
- e **dr**________ the car
- f **fl**________ of sheep
- g **fr**________ of the house
- h **gl**________ of light
- i **gr**________ of visitors
- j **pl**________ the crop

2 **Circle** the **two real words** in each group of three.

- a prompt, prowl, pril
- b scamp, scild, scoop
- c scrub, screech, scred
- d skate, skup, skipper
- e slack, slope, slint
- f smile, smig, small
- g snack, snurp, sneer
- h spend, speck, spiw
- i splut, split, splay
- j spruy, spring, sprout
- k stive, stale, storm
- l stride, string, strang
- m swept, swinm, swish
- n thrust, throat, thrat

3 **Build three words** for each of the **initial blends** shown.

- a (sw) ________ ________ ________
- b (sk) ________ ________ ________
- c (bl) ________ ________ ________
- d (cl) ________ ________ ________
- e (fl) ________ ________ ________
- f (br) ________ ________ ________
- g (cr) ________ ________ ________
- h (dr) ________ ________ ________

☞ Answers on page 121

Final blends

● **Say** the words. ● **Listen** for the final blends. ● **Complete** the activities.

bun **ch**	du **ck**	a **ct**	ra **ft**	cou **gh**	ye **lp**
bo **lt**	la **mp**	ha **nd**	ri **ng**	tru **nk**	te **nt**
we **pt**	fi **sh**	ma **sk**	fi **st**	mou **th**	

1 **Complete** the phrases using words built with the **final blends** indicated in **bold**.

a sandwiches for _______**ch**

b _______**ck** and roll music

c a _______**ct** answer

d a _______**ft** of grass

e a quick _____**lp** of water

f the rubbish _______**mp**

g a neat _______**nd** castle

h a ___**ng** piece of rope

i a _______**nk** page

j the _______**nt** pencil

2 **Circle** the words with the **final blends** from the box above. **Write** a **new word** for each of the blends.

a spent _______________

b slept _______________

c colt _______________

d little _______________

e task _______________

f first _______________

g month _______________

h tough _______________

3 **Complete words** with the **final blends** indicated in **bold** to finish these sentences.

a The horse will ________**mp** his feet on the concrete floor.

b There was _________**ch** more for the children to finish.

c They will ________**ft** the table into the other room.

d All the jewels were placed in the main ________**lt**.

e The parcel was tied together with ________**ng**.

f The collection of old books had been placed in the _________**nk**.

g She _________**pt** quietly into the room.

h They _________**st** their fishing lines into the deep water.

i It was difficult to decide if the prisoner was telling the ________**th**.

j The explorers found it difficult to travel across the _________**gh** country.

Answers on page 121

Consonant sounds

How much do you know?

1 **Add** a suitable **single consonant** to the following.

___elow ___azzle ___orced ___azed
___idden ___ewel ___oala ___inger
___asked ___eedle ___ebble ___each
___atin ___omato ___acant ___aiting
___owl ___oned

2 **Add** a **single consonant sound** to these letters to **make** a **word**.

- **a** ? ave ________________
- **b** ? ip ________________
- **c** ? ame ________________
- **d** ? ent ________________
- **e** ? ine ________________
- **f** ? ole ________________

3 **Form words** using the **combination sounds** in **bold** by **adding letters** in the spaces.

- **a** The fire will ____**or**____ the side of the building.
- **b** Because of the ____**ou**____, the graziers had to purchase stock feed.
- **c** The bathroom ________**ow** was broken when hit by the ball.
- **d** They heard the ____**ir**____ of the newly hatched birds.
- **e** They had been ____**aw**____ on the paper for some time.

4 **Circle three real words** in each group of four.

- **a** spilling, spire, spoiling, spoort
- **b** grinned, greatly, greting, gristle
- **c** climber, cleanser, cluss, clench
- **d** sweater, surples, swimmer, swampy
- **e** flannel, flant, flavour, fleecy
- **f** bracket, branches, briker, breathe

5 **Complete** the **words** by adding letters to the **bold** letters to finish these sentences.

- **a** The money was hidden in the ________**mp** of bushes.
- **b** All the provisions for the picnic were placed in the _____**sk**_____.
- **c** The people will _________**ct** one of these candidates on Saturday.
- **d** The film director said the _________**pt** was a very interesting one.
- **e** The thirsty children were ________**lp**________ down the cool drinks.
- **f** All the materials were ________**ft**________ from the building site.

Answers on page 121

Review test 1

1 **Circle** the words with a **long *a*** or ***e*** sound. **Underline** the words with a **short *a*** or ***e*** sound.

shape	always	believe	dentist	prize	shining
voyage	grateful	injury	scene	admire	equal
average	attend	silver	twine	sheep	dingo
Sunday	crack	spilt	family	tonight	educate

2 **Use each** of the **letters** in the long box with those in the circle to build a word with the **short *e*** sound.

f l m t tr sp pret

end

__________ __________ __________

__________ __________ __________ __________

3 **Use each** of the **letters** in the long box with those in the circle to build a word with the **long *e*** sound.

m s n bl pl tr

eat

__________ __________ __________

__________ __________ __________

4 **Make rhyming words** for the words below.

a gold __________

b coat __________

5 **Add** the ***u* sound** to complete these words. Mark **S** (short) or **L** (long) in the box to describe the sound.

ad___lt	☐	f___nny	☐	g___llies	☐
r___ler	☐	d___ring	☐	fort___ne	☐
inj___ry	☐	r___bbish	☐	___ncles	☐

6 **Select** a **suitable word** from the box to complete each sentence. Mark **S** or **L** in the box to describe the sound in **bold**.

h**ea**rty sn**a**kes s**ei**zing **i**tem c**oa**stal stat**ue**

a The animal was __________ ☐ the food in its jaws.

b An __________ ☐ of clothing was left on the ground.

c The __________ ☐ showers continued into the night.

d The small __________ ☐ in the garden had been damaged.

e The athletes had all eaten a __________ ☐ breakfast.

☞ Answers on page 121

Review test 1

7 **Circle** the words with the **hard *c*** or ***g*** sound. **Underline** the words with the **soft *c*** or ***g*** sound.

corncob	gamble	gasket	corridor	coast	gesture
gazebo	civilian	gangster	genius	gargle	certain
cereal	consumer	gentle	ceremony	central	cover

8 **Add** a suitable **single consonant** to the following.

___eaching	___urial	___oisture	___orrier
___onesty	___anteen	___azed	___itness
___eneral	___unior	___urvey	___eenly
___aused	___ansom	___oughen	

9 **Add combination sounds** from the box to **complete** the **words**.

ow	ir	oi	al	er
or	aw	ar	ur	

l_____est	spr_____l	c_____cle	sub_____b
h_____dship	w_____se	p_____son	c_____ves
t_____el	m_____mur	gr_____th	

10 **Build four words** using each of the blends shown.

a (sp) __________ __________ __________ __________

b (st) __________ __________ __________ __________

c (fl) __________ __________ __________ __________

d (tr) __________ __________ __________ __________

e (tw) __________ __________ __________ __________

11 **Complete** the **words** using the **endings** in the box.

lb	pt	lk	mp	ct
ft	lt	sk	st	

a The workers swe_____ the path carefully.

b The huge stu_____ was removed from the ground.

c All the team members were pleased with the resu_____.

d The si_____en cloth was very beautiful.

e The stranger was a suspe_____ in the robbery.

f The severe fro_____ killed many of the new plants.

12 **Build four words** using each of the **final blends** shown.

a (nt) ____

b (nk) ____

c (mp) ____

Answers on page 121

Puzzle time 1

Crossword 1

Across

4 common type of snack
5 person who hunts
7 used to tie up something
8 trip or journey
10 moved from side to side
12 sounds made when amused
15 fastest pace of a horse
16 native Australian dog
17 person who begs
19 opposite of *deep*

Down

1 something that lights
2 almost or not quite
3 look with wonder
6 the centre
9 field or grazing area
10 step out strongly
11 opposite of *kind*
13 welcoming
14 wreck or damage
18 terrible or horrible

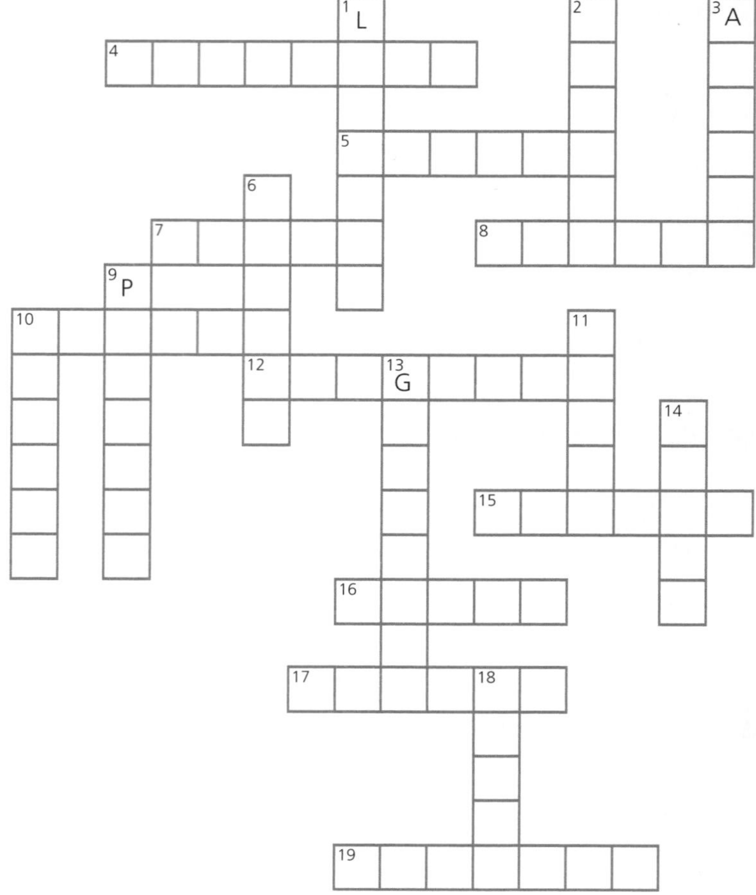

Wordsearch 1

There are ten words from Chapter 1 in this word search. They can be horizontal, vertical or diagonal. The words begin with the letters shown in the box on the left.

w
f
b
h
s
g
n
c
c
m

G F R W M W A D I X U H C M B
Q X S V E L X K D B C J R J F
O C S G X J I X J A B E T E U
Z L B Y Q T H F O D G D N O V
K D D J P Y A C F A P L W B E
R S M H H E W A J I E F S I Y
K C I A K G K U W B R A I N E
Q X A L N E E D L E O S N L L
G J W V V N G A S E S Z I B F
F F R A G E A C U K G F S R F
A K S Y N H R R O B I F Q L Z
M Y I W L T T G F U M O V I E
I A E V N I E C R T P A L Y D
L O R F I O L D A I K L L S W
Y W Z N E C S E K P Y V E G Y

Answers on page 122

2 Spelling strategies

Strategy 1 Visual patterns – same shape

The letters of a word form a shape, with some letters extending upwards and some downwards. In this strategy you will practise identifying words that are the **same shape** and have the **same number of letters**.

Examples

duck – dust
park – part
drive – drove
much – most

1 **Find** the **words** from the box with the **same shape** as the words below.

a hard ________ ________
b hope ________ ________
c dried ________ ________
d horse ________ ________
e month ________ ________

taps	trail	lips
live	own	lank
mouth	loose	drink
hand	lurch	mud
earth	teams	

2 From the box **find eight pairs** of words that are the **same shape**. The first of each pair is shown in **bold**. Write the pairs below.

making	swamp	liking	after	alone
dream	**often**	**depart**	ale	depend
six	happen	beads	**steam**	**window**
hears	winter	**wooden**	**castles**	wrap
butter	smother	mantis	twelve	eatery

____
____
____

3 **Use your dictionary** to find two other words with the **same shape** as the ones below.

a weary ________ ________
b straw ________ ________
c whom ________ ________
d power ________ ________
e voice ________ ________
f final ________ ________

Quick check

The following pairs of words have the **same shape**. Indicate **T** (true) or **F** (false).

1 guest, gully ____
2 flour, blame ____
3 trick, brand ____
4 group, grief ____
5 cement, silent ____
6 obtain, unless ____
7 launch, bitter ____
8 treat, field ____

Answers on page 122

Strategy 2 Visual patterns – same pattern

In this strategy you will practise identifying words with the **same** or **very similar patterns**. The pairs of words may have the same or very similar **shape** as well as the same or very similar **beginnings, middle letters** or **endings**.

Examples

force – fence (same)	grain – grave (same)
cattle – baffle (similar)	gleam – steam (similar)
begged – rigged (similar)	pebble – wobble (similar)

1 **Find two words** from the box with the **same** or **similar pattern** as those below.

a watch __________ __________
b setting __________ __________
c winter __________ __________
d white __________ __________
e shout __________ __________
f stand __________ __________

yelling	short	whole
about	cooler	wedding
sister	match	latch
pretty	sweep	stick
while	bright	valet
rush	twins	start

2 From the box **choose eight pairs** of **words** that have the **same** or very **similar patterns**.

smoke	hammer	found	shoving	dinner
closing	lashes	smile	people	load
cannot	putting	evening	jotting	carrot
morning	never	motor	bound	nurse
old	lucky	dishes	park	card

____

____

____

____

3 Using your dictionary, **find two words** with the **same** or very **similar pattern** as the ones below.

a farmer __________ __________ b cutting __________ __________
c lunch __________ __________ d beside __________ __________

Quick check

The following pairs of words have the **same** or **very similar patterns**. Indicate **T** (true) or **F** (false).

1 house, loose ____ 2 garden, ladder ____
3 hurry, merry ____ 4 hopped, slide ____
5 storm, stern ____ 6 sorry, lobby ____
7 thank, think ____ 8 happen, meddle ____

Answers on page 122

Strategy 3 Visual patterns – words containing smaller words

In this strategy, you will practise using **words that contain smaller words**.

Examples

f**low**er	be**long**s	**teach**er
b**row**n	**bask**et	s**had**e

1 **Find** the **word(s)** contained in the **longer words** below.

a believe ____________ b shallow ____________
c careless ____________ d weary ____________
e favourite ____________ f breath ____________
g important ____________ h broadcast ____________
i leather ____________ j steal ____________

2 **Match** the **small words** from the box with the **longer words** that contain them.

hall	owe	sip	tie	ten
her	own	tin	row	list
and	ear	as	tea	am

a blister ____________________ b continent ____________________
c attend ____________________ d power ____________________
e steam ____________________ f township ____________________
g shallow ____________________ h burrow ____________________
i search ____________________ j handy ____________________

3 **Add small words** from the box to make longer words.

had	tent	urn	art	hall
here	cell	tee	rig	tart

a p____________icle b t____________fore
c ex____________ent d ir____________ate
e f____________ish f s____________ing
g s____________l h s____________ow
i at____________ion j s____________le

Quick check

Choose the **small words** from the box to build **longer words**.

our	form	rear	ten	oar	ease	air	ash

1 b______der 2 sen______ces 3 f______ies
4 d______y 5 d______ing 6 m______n
7 per______er 8 l______d

Answers on page 122

Strategy 4 Exploring homonyms – 1

In this strategy you will practise using homonyms. A **homonym** is a word that has the **same sound** as another word but has **different spelling and meaning**.

Examples

berry (fruit) — **bury** (cover up)
flour (used to cook with) — **flower** (part of plant)
board (timber) — **bored** (not interested)

1 **Select homonyms** from the box for the words listed below.

a arc ________	**b** chews ________	bawl	grown
c due ________	**d** bight ________	dew	fourth
e dear ________	**f** bread ________	sell	ark
g find ________	**h** base ________	claws	deer
i feat ________	**j** cell ________	bite	bass
k creak ________	**l** bough ________	choose	bow
m carat ________	**n** crews ________	eight	dye
o ate ________	**p** fair ________	fined	creek
q foul ________	**r** blew ________	fare	carrot
s clause ________	**t** die ________	cruise	feet
u ball ________	**v** forth ________	blue	fowl
w groan ________	**x** berth ________	bred	birth

2 **Choose** the **correct homonym** from the brackets to complete the sentence.

a They were in the store to ______________ new clothes. (by, buy)
b It was sold at a very ______________ price. (cheep, cheap)
c They dived on the ______________ reef all day. (choral, coral)
d The ____________________________ had lived in the house for years. (boarder, border)
e The tall ______________ tree was growing well. (beach, beech)
f Sharon has ______________ to that show many times. (bean, been)
g The ______________ of wool was on the truck. (bail, bale)
h Did she ______________ the cup this morning? (break, brake)
i The wine was stored in the ______________. (seller, cellar)
j The youth will ______________ a lot of money this year. (urn, earn)

3 **Add** the necessary letters to **complete** these **homonyms**.

a draft drau__________ **b** ewes u__________ **c** fate f__________
d flaw flo__________ **e** frays phr__________ **f** frieze fre__________
g nor gn__________ **h** great gra__________ **i** guest gue__________
j hair ha__________

☞ Answers on pages 122–123

Strategy 4 Exploring homonyms – 2

In this strategy you will practise using homonyms. A **homonym** is a word that has the **same sound** as another word but has **different spelling and meaning**.

Examples

course (track or path) — **coarse** (rough)
hoard (to stock up) — **horde** (large group)
plain (ordinary) — **plane** (aircraft)

1 **Select homonyms** from the box for the words below.

a heal ________ b rays ________
c sees ________ d sort ________
e idle ________ f war ________
g pole ________ h wood ________
i which ________ j loan ________
k tide ________ l praise ________
m one ________ n throne ________
o loot ________ p side ________
q suite ________ r him ________
s toad ________ t peer ________
u their ________ v lain ________
w wail ________ x missed ________

won	sighed
towed	wore
hymn	lute
lane	lone
raise	witch
there	sought
poll	tied
thrown	pier
whale	prays
heel	sweet
would	mist
idol	seas

2 **Choose** the **correct homonym** from the brackets to complete the sentence.

a She will ________ a hole into the timber. (boar, bore)
b The ________ was used to prepare the food. (greater, grater)
c All the ________ was delivered yesterday. (mail, male)
d The shoes were ________ in the factory. (made, maid)
e The athlete ________ up and down before the event. (paste, paced)
f The wall was a very ________ colour. (pail, pale)
g The racing boats rounded the marker ________. (boy, buoy)
h The ________ in the river was very strong. (currant, current)
i She will try to ________ a taxi now. (hail, hale)
j All the ________ pipes had been damaged. (led, lead)

3 **Add** the necessary letters to **complete** the **homonyms**.

a prise pri________ b pedal ped________ c seem se________
d road ro________ e stake st________ f weighed wa________
g wait wei________ h straight str________ i right wr________
j rain rei________

Answers on page 123

Strategy 5 Exploring homographs – 1

In this strategy you will practise using homographs. A **homograph** is a word that is **spelt the same** as another word but has a **different meaning**.

Examples

bark
- a sound made by a dog
- the outer covering of a tree

beam
- a length of wood or concrete
- the widest part of a ship
- a ray of light

1 **Complete** the **sentences** using the words in the box.

bank	fair	form	match	ring
calf	fast	ground	prune	

a The young girl had shiny __________ hair.

b All the family went to the spring __________.

c She fell down the __________ of the creek.

d All the money was placed in the safe at the __________.

e His __________ muscle was injured during training.

f Did you see the newborn __________ in the yard?

g It was difficult to dig up the hard __________.

h The machine __________ the coffee beans.

i She lit the __________ at the cave entrance.

j Does this card __________ the one on the table?

k The __________ and the other dried fruits were on the plate.

l The gardener will __________ the shrubs well.

m The delivery worker will __________ the doorbell.

n The __________ that he bought was placed in the case.

o During the religious event the people will __________ for seven days.

p The car that crashed was travelling too __________.

q They filled in the __________ at the local bank.

r The correct __________ of address for the official is 'Your Honour'.

2 **Match** each **group of meanings** with a **word** from the box. **Write** the word in the grid.

case	drill	grain	lean	mean
crop	felt	hide	light	perch

a a box or container a charge against someone in court	**b** a tool for boring holes training with repeated exercise
c selfish or stingy the average	**d** product growing in the soil to cut short
e something to roost on a type of fish	**f** direction of fibres in wood small hard seed
g skin of an animal to keep from view	**h** very thin rest against
i a type of material touched	**j** used for traffic control to start a fire

☞ Answers on page 123

Strategy 5 Exploring homographs – 2

In this strategy you will practise using homographs. A **homograph** is a word that is **spelt the same** as another word but has a **different meaning**.

Examples

blow
- a hard hit (noun)
- moving air (noun)
- destroy with explosives (verb)

table
- a piece of furniture (noun)
- a list of items or chapters (noun)
- to put out in parliament for discussion (verb)

1 **Provide** an **additional meaning** for each of the words below.

a	bear	to put up with	______________
b	crane	to stretch in order to see	______________
c	crow	to boast about	______________
d	fine	good quality	______________
e	pitch	to throw	______________
f	range	variety	______________
g	rest	what remains	______________
h	scale	to climb a mountain	______________
i	steer	to guide	______________
j	train	a form of transport	______________

2 **Complete** the **sentences** using the words in the box.

club grate sign stock suit

a On the gate was a large ______________ telling visitors to keep out.

b He was asked to ______________ the paper at the office.

c All the ______________ had been placed in the warehouse.

d The ______________ of the rifle had been damaged.

e Jason bought a new ______________ for the special evening.

f I do not think that colour will ______________ you.

g The ______________ was blocked with leaves after the storm.

h This sound will ______________ on my nerves after a while.

i The warrior used a huge ______________ in battle.

j Many of the residents joined the fitness ______________.

3 **Write two different meanings** for each of these words.

a bill ______________ ______________

b long ______________ ______________

c ruler ______________ ______________

d rock ______________ ______________

e spell ______________ ______________

Answers on page 123

Visual patterns, homonyms, homographs

1 The following pairs have the same shape. **Indicate T** (true) or **F** (false).

a craft, dwell ____ **b** blade, throw ____
c skull, still ____ **d** order, irate ____
e wreck, smack ____ **f** match, wrote ____
g ditch, latch ____ **h** cluck, clout ____

2 The following words have the same or very similar patterns. **Indicate T** (true) or **F** (false).

a perch, joint ____ **b** train, frame ____
c hamper, jumper ____ **d** ground, quests ____
e capital, cashier ____ **f** wallow, settee ____

3 **Use small words** from the box to make **longer words**.

gain	lot	get	rat	mat	cat	ink	owe

a cli__________e **b** b__________r **c** a__________st
d al__________ment **e** lo__________e **f** pi__________e
g s__________ing **h** tar__________ng

4 **Select homonyms** from the box for the words listed below.

a laps __________ **b** made __________
c pail __________ **d** pedal __________
e pole __________ **f** praise __________
g stare __________ **h** tacks __________
i through __________ **j** vale __________

peddle	tax
lapse	threw
stair	pale
prays	veil
maid	poll

5 **Add** the necessary letters to **complete homonyms** of the words in **bold**.

a **rapped** wr__________ **b** **toe** t__________
c **aisle** is__________ **d** **bold** bow__________
e **cereal** se__________ **f** **site** si__________
g **flea** fl__________ **h** **sole** so__________

6 **Match** each **group of meanings** with a **word** from the box. **Write** the word in the grid.

spoke	hail	file	park	row	cross

a to arrange in sets or groups a steel tool	**b** part of a wheel said something
c small pieces of ice to shout or call	**d** line of things or people propel a small boat
e shape made by two straight lines being annoyed	**f** leave a car beside the road public area with trees

Answers on page 123

Strategy 6 Exploring word families – 1

In this strategy you will practise **building word families**. Different **endings** are added to make new words.

Simply add endings				Drop silent e before endings				
assist	-s	➠	assists	admir**e**	admir	-es	➠	admires
	-ed	➠	assisted			-ed	➠	admired
	-ing	➠	assisting			-ing	➠	admiring
	-ant	➠	assistant			-er	➠	admirer
	-ance	➠	assistance			-ation	➠	admiration
						-able	➠	admirable

1 **Use** these **words** and **endings** to **build word families**.

a breath -e, -es, -ed, -ing, -less

____
____
____
____
____

b graz**e** -es, -ed, -ing, -ier

____
____
____
____
____

c inspect -s, -ed, -ing, -ion, -or

____
____
____
____
____

2 **Read** these words and endings. **Use** the **appropriate word** from the family to complete the sentences.

a prepar**e** -es, -ed, -ing, -ations, -atory

i The mountain climbers were making ____________________ for the difficult climb.

ii Much of the ____________________ work had been done before dawn.

b strang**e** -ely, -er, -est

i The crowd at the football game was ____________________ silent.

ii It was the ____________________ noise I had ever heard.

c divi**de** -des, -ded, -ding, -sion, -sible, -sor

i He found that the number was evenly ____________________ by two, four and eight.

ii The ____________________ of the money into eleven shares took several hours.

☞ Answers on page 123

Strategy 6 Exploring word families – 2

In this strategy you will practise **building word families**. New **beginnings** can also be added to change the meaning.

comfort: *un-* is added only to the endings in bold type	**apply: *re-* is added only to endings in bold type**
un- comfort -s -ed -ing **-able** **-ably**	re- appl**y** **-ies** **-ied** **-ying** **-ication** -icable
comforts, comforted, comforting, comfortable, comfortably, uncomfortable, uncomfortably	applies, applied, applying, application, applicable, reapply, reapplied, reapplying, reapplication

1 **Use** these **word endings** and **beginnings** to build the word families.

a dis- tast**e** -es
-ed
-ing
-ily
-eful

____
____
____
____
____
____

b un- eas**e** -es
-ed
-ing
-ily

____
____
____
____
____
____

c re- suppl**y** **-ies**
-ied
-ying
-ier

____
____
____
____
____
____

2 **Read** these words and endings. **Use** the **appropriate word** to complete the sentences.

a re- settl**e** **-es**
-ed
-ing
-er
-ement

i The first ________________ was established there in the 1820s.
ii The villagers took many years to ____________________ the valley after the earthquake.

b un- attract-s
-ed
-ing
-ion
-ive
ively

i The family visited the famous tourist ____________________.
ii The prince and princess were very ____________________ dressed for the ceremony.

3 **Add** any other **endings**. **Write** the **new words** your endings have formed.

a depart -s
-ed
-ing

____
____
____

b un- employ -s
-ed
-ing

____
____
____

c in- complet**e** -es
-ed
-ing

____
____
____

☞ Answers on page 123

Strategy 7 Letter clusters

In this strategy you will practise building words from **groups of letters**.

Examples
be + hold + er = beholder
mag + net + ic = magnetic
em + ploy + able = employable

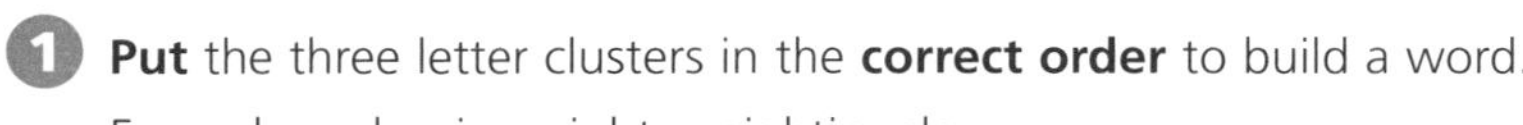

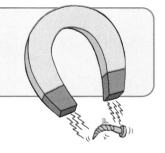

1 **Put** the three letter clusters in the **correct order** to build a word.

Example: gale in night = nightingale

a er num acy ______

b es tries tap ______

c ping ship wor ______

d able pass im ______

e able tol er ______

f cheat wind er ______

g keep score er ______

h pend ex able ______

2 **Add *de*** to the following pairs of letter clusters. **Write** the **new words**.

a ed, form ______

b flat, ed ______

c ly, cent ______

d ite, fin ______

e ful, light ______

f press, ion ______

g ing, let ______

h ure, part ______

3 In each case two letter clusters have been provided. **Add** a third **letter cluster** to **make** a **word** in the box. **Write** the missing letter cluster and the word.

a ed, sign ___ ______

b ous, der ___ ______

c ion, act ___ ______

d cy, va ___ ______

e ed, over ___ ______

f ten, ise ___ ______

g or, ject ___ ______

h ence, pre___ ______

i ance, per___ ______

tenderise	vacancy
performance	objector
reaction	preference
overjoyed	resigned
ponderous	

4 **Combine** the letter clusters to **form words**. Use your dictionary to check them.

a nite gel ig ______

b tine pen tur ______

c viron ment en ______

d er dis ord ______

e path sym y ______

f it mon or ______

g loc ed at ______

h ent tim sen ______

☞ Answers on pages 123–124

Strategy 8 Exploring synonyms – 1

In this strategy you will practise using synonyms. A **synonym** is a word that means the **same** or nearly the same **as another word**.

Examples

leave — depart
eager — keen
foolish — stupid
strong — powerful

1 **Match** the words in the box to those in the circle. **Write** the pairs of **synonyms**.

dismal
abruptly
display
bought
burglary
broad
conceal
absurd
brutal
applaud

clap wide
ridiculous unhappy
cruel show suddenly
hide theft
purchased

______________________ ______________________
______________________ ______________________
______________________ ______________________
______________________ ______________________
______________________ ______________________

2 **Complete** the **synonyms** for the words in **bold**.

a **stick** ad__________
b **begin** com__________
c **surprise** aston__________
d **wages** earn__________
e **apparent** obvi__________
f **polite** cour__________
g **awkward** clu__________
h **huge** im__________

3 **Match** the **words** to the **synonym stems** in the box. **Write** the **synonyms**.

of_____
sol_____
tas_____
val_____
care_____
free_____
holi_____
bui_____
str_____
proh_____
sin_____
stu_____

a vacation __________________
b flavour __________________
c caution __________________
d precious __________________
e liberty __________________
f construct __________________
g scholar __________________
h serious __________________
i forbid __________________
j peculiar __________________
k frequently __________________
l earnest __________________

Answers on page 124

Strategy 8 Exploring synonyms – 2

In this strategy you will practise using synonyms. A **synonym** is a word that means the **same** or nearly the same **as another word**.

Examples

certain — sure
usual — common
remark — comment
beautiful — attractive

1 **Match** the words in the box with those in the circle. **Write** the pairs of **synonyms**.

reveal	holy
notify	molten
extensive	dangerous
obstruct	remember
lively	shake

advise
disclose perilous
large vigorous melted
sacred hinder
recollect tremble

________________ ________________
________________ ________________
________________ ________________
________________ ________________
________________ ________________

2 **Complete** the **synonyms** for these words.

a prosperous weal________ **b** decorated ador________
c resemblance like________ **d** loving affect________
e keep pre________ **f** colossal imm________

3 **Match** the words with the **synonym stems** in the box. **Write** the **synonyms**.

frag_____	move_____	myster_____	comp_____
narrat_____	fore_____	fu_____	necess_____
fri_____	spect_____	weari_____	amus_____

a onlooker ________________ **b** story ________________
c strange ________________ **d** comrade ________________
e motion ________________ **f** predict ________________
g entertainment ________________ **h** part ________________
i humorous ________________ **j** essential ________________
k tiredness ________________ **l** forced ________________

Answers on page 124

Strategy 9 Exploring antonyms – 1

In this strategy you will practise using antonyms. An **antonym** is a word that means the **opposite** or nearly the opposite of **another word**.

Examples

foolish — sensible	cease — commence
heavy — light	backwards — forwards

1 **Match** the words in the left-hand box to their **antonyms** in the circle.

imports	valuable
mourn	wealthy
cruelty	conceal
inferior	beneath
briskly	broad

slowly rejoice
exports above
kindness poor
worthless reveal
narrow superior

______________________ ______________________
______________________ ______________________
______________________ ______________________
______________________ ______________________
______________________ ______________________

2 **Complete** the **antonyms** for these words.

a	accurate	care______	b	immense	sm______
c	ascend	des______	d	urban	rur______
e	dull	brill______	f	lazy	industr______
g	prohibit	all______	h	cheap	expen______

3 **Match** the **words** with the **antonym stems** in the box. **Write** the **antonyms**.

vert______	incr______	nat______	slow______
hat______	weak______	fin______	nega______
pres______	cheer______	fier______	str______

a	strengthen	______	b	positive	______
c	horizontal	______	d	absence	______
e	artificial	______	f	commence	______
g	dismal	______	h	decrease	______
i	abruptly	______	j	tame	______
k	familiar	______	l	love	______

☞ Answers on page 124

Strategy 9 Exploring antonyms – 2

In this strategy you will practise using antonyms. An **antonym** is a word that means the **opposite** or nearly the opposite of **another word**.

Examples

proud — humble
least — most
friend — enemy
difficult — simple

1 **Select antonyms** from the box to match the words below.

inactive	barren	mobile	disperse	defeat	scarcity
uncommon	small	pleasure	majority	comedy	recollect
minimum	foolish	collect	beginning	important	graceful

a abundance ____________
b assemble ____________
c awkward ____________
d vigorous ____________
e victory ____________
f stationary ____________
g forget ____________
h conclusion ____________
i maximum ____________
j immense ____________
k distribute ____________
l intelligent ____________
m minority ____________
n tragedy ____________
o trivial ____________
p fertile ____________

2 **Complete** the **antonym pairs** by adding the required letters.

a absent pre________
b construction dest________
c descent as________
d aboard ash________
e addition subt________
f buried unear________
g external int________
h courteous r________

3 **Match** the **antonym stems** in the box to the words below. **Write** the **antonyms** beside their words.

friend_____	freq_____	la_____	bor_____
change_____	ser_____	temp_____	amat_____
repul_____	contra_____	sens_____	trans_____

a occasionally ____________
b interesting ____________
c attraction ____________
d permanent ____________
e hostility ____________
f humorous ____________
g professional ____________
h constant ____________
i energetic ____________
j opaque ____________
k expansion ____________
l ridiculous ____________

Answers on page 124

Strategy 9 Exploring antonyms – 3

In this strategy you will practise using antonyms. An **antonym** is a word that means the **opposite** or nearly the opposite of **another word**. Often a **prefix** is used to create the antonym. A prefix is a **syllable placed in front of a word**.

Examples

agree — **dis**agree
legal — **il**legal
common — **un**common
place — **mis**place

1 **Use** the **prefix *dis-*** to form **antonyms** of these words.

a advantage ____________ **b** allow ____________
c appear ____________ **d** approve ____________
e content ____________ **f** continue ____________
g like ____________ **h** obedient ____________
i obey ____________ **j** organise ____________

2 **Use *in-*** or ***un-*** as a **prefix** to form **antonyms** of these words.

a aware ____________ **b** selfish ____________
c skilful ____________ **d** clothe ____________
e sane ____________ **f** audible ____________
g correct ____________ **h** happy ____________
i faithful ____________ **j** necessary ____________

3 **Use** one of the **prefixes *mis-*, *il-*, *im-*** or ***ir-*** to write **antonyms** for the given words.

a religious ____________ **b** behave ____________
c patient ____________ **d** fortune ____________
e pure ____________ **f** represent ____________
g mature ____________ **h** legal ____________
i understand ____________ **j** regular ____________
k mortal ____________ **l** legible ____________

4 **Add** the appropriate **prefix** (***in-*, *dis-*, *de-*, *mis-*, *un-*, *il-*, *im-*** or ***ir-***) to the words below.

a ____believe **b** ____centralise
c ____connect **d** ____worthy
e ____trust **f** ____reverent
g ____polite **h** ____please
i ____order **j** ____movable
k ____convenient **l** ____grateful
m ____honest **n** ____logical

☞ Answers on page 124

Word families, letter clusters, synonyms, antonyms

How much do you know?

1 **Study** the endings. The prefix in **bold** is only used with the **bold** endings. **Use** the most **appropriate words** to complete the sentences.

un- reason -s, -ed, -ing, **-able**, **-ably**

a The cost was so ____________________ that the customer would not buy the article.

b Because the car was ____________________ priced it was soon sold.

2 Use the word and the endings to **build** the **word family**.

en- courag**e** -eous ____________________

-eously ____________________

-es ____________________

-ed ____________________

-ing ____________________

3 **Rearrange** and **combine** the letter clusters to form true words.

a ing volt re

____

b less list ness

____

c er pol ish

____

d form mis in

____

4 **Match** the **synonym stems** in the box with the words below. **Write** the **synonyms**.

obstin____ onlook____ ann_____ waste______

a extravagant ____________________

b tell ____________________

c stubborn ____________________

d spectator ____________________

5 **Complete** the **antonyms** for these words by adding the required letters.

a assent dis__________

b ugly attra__________

c humane bru__________

d kindle exting__________

e voluntary compul_______

f diminish incr__________

g precede succ__________

h guilt innoc__________

6 **Add** the appropriate **prefix** ***in-***, ***dis-***, ***mis-***, ***un-***, ***il-***, ***im-*** or ***ir-*** to the words below to form **antonyms** of the word given.

a _________possess

b _________comfortable

c _________safe

d _________understand

e _________engage

f _________perfect

g _________prove

h _________satisfactory

i _________polite

j _________audible

Answers on page 124

Strategy 10 Using a dictionary – 1

In this strategy you use the following activities to **sharpen your dictionary skills**.

1 **Look** at these **pairs of words**. Does the first word come **before** or **after** the second word in a dictionary? Write *before* or *after*.

a branch, bulb ____________________ b chop, city ____________________

c deck, dash ____________________ d end, egg ____________________

e monkey, molten ____________________ f pewter, petty ____________________

2 **Which word** in these sets would come **last** in a dictionary? **Write** it in the space.

a abrupt, aerial, actual, aloud ____________________

b burial, bargain, become, bomb ____________________

c clank, cigar, catch, chapel ____________________

3 **Rewrite** these sets of words **in alphabetical order**.

a amber, advice, actual, agate, alike

____

b errand, effort, excite, endure, ease

____

4 The **meanings** of these words are correct. **Check** in a dictionary and **answer T** (true) or **F** (false).

a **absurd**: stupid _____ b **bashful**: terrible _____

c **earnest**: serious _____ d **damage**: fix _____

5 The following sets of words should have been in **alphabetical order**. **Write** the first word that is **out of place**.

a aim, allow, ample, ape, agile ____________________

b bawl, behind, burrow, blade, bonfire ____________________

c camel, charge, cricket, city, clasp ____________________

6 **Write** the **meanings** of the following words.

a fleece ____

b groove ____

c hyacinth ____

d imitate ____

e legend ____

7 The **key word** at the top left-hand corner of a dictionary page shows the **first word** on that page. In a dictionary these key words are at the top of the pages noted.

bandit (page 11) bang (page 12) bath (page 13) beet (page 14)

On **which page** would these words be?

a beach _____ b bawl _____ c banner _____

d banana _____ e belt _____ f bashful _____

☞ Answers on page 125

Strategy 10 Using a dictionary – 2

In this strategy you use the following activities to **sharpen your dictionary skills**.

1 **Write** the **word** from the list that comes **before** the word in **bold**.

a husband, huddle, hustle **humour** ____________________

b inhabit, impudent, impress **improve** ____________________

c launch, lawn, laze **laundry** ____________________

d migrant, million, millet **military** ____________________

e notorious, notable, notion **notice** ____________________

2 Does the **first word** come **before** or **after** the **second word** in a dictionary? **Write** *before* or *after*.

a feature, feasible ______________ b garnish, garrison ______________

c harvest, harpoon ______________ d indicate, indelible ______________

e jungle, justice ______________ f magazine, manager ______________

3 **Write** the following sets of words in **alphabetical order**.

a nautical, notion, natural, narrate

____

b pensive, peninsula, penguin, pension

____

c qualm, quarry, quantity, quality

____

4 In your dictionary **find a word** that comes **between these pairs of words**.

a retire, revenge ____________________

b sample, sandwich ____________________

c thick, thrust ____________________

d vermin, vertical ____________________

5 **Find** the words that **mean** the following. **Use** the **stem** given as a guide.

a very graceful: dai______ b to announce: dec______

c to fear: dre______ d a short sword: sci______

e a tomb: sep______ f to stay for a time: soj______

6 **Use** your **dictionary** to **complete** the following **statements**.

a A *cairn* is a ____________________

b A *calamity* is an event ____________________

c A *cenotaph* is a ____________________

d A *soliloquy* is a ____________________

e A *frontispiece* is a ____________________

Answers on page 125

Review test 2

1 The following pairs of words have the **same shape**. **Mark** each **T** (true) or **F** (false).

a panic, glued _____ **b** evade, ankle _____ **c** amber, motor _____

d stolen, whales _____ **e** stoking, skilful _____ **f** resent, musing _____

2 Use the words in the box to **write six pairs of words** that have the **same** or **very similar patterns**.

sword	annul	scroll	smooth
trick	drawl	torture	marked
rocket	merrily	perform	variety

________________ ________________

________________ ________________

________________ ________________

3 **Combine** the groups of letters in the circle with the incomplete words in the box to **write true words**.

con_____tion	par_____able	en_____ment
jeal_____y	for_____ity	de_____ite
re_____tivate	neigh_____hood	

mal ous
vic fin bour
ac rich
don

________________ ________________

________________ ________________

________________ ________________

________________ ________________

4 **Add** the necessary letters to **complete** the pairs of **homonyms**.

a bald baw__________ **b** barque ba__________

c fir f__________ **d** cheque ch__________

e curb k__________ **f** preys pr__________

g witch wh__________ **h** tail ta__________

5 **Use** the **words** in the box to **complete** the **sentences**.

vault	firm	litter	stern

a The officer spoke with a __________________ voice.

b The __________________ of the vessel was damaged.

c Here is the __________________ of kittens.

d Do not leave __________________ in the grounds.

e This ________________ manufactures farming equipment.

f The fruit on the tree was still quite __________________.

g The gymnast was able to ______________ the box with ease.

h All the money had been kept in the __________________.

☞ Answers on page 125

Review test 2

6 **Use** this **word beginning** and the **endings** to build the **word family**. The **bold** prefix is only used with the **bold** endings.

en- forc**e** | **-es** ______
-ed ______
-ing ______
-eful ______
-efully ______

7 **Check** the word beginnings and endings. **Use** the most **appropriate words** to **complete** the **sentences**.

un- prepar**e** -es, **-ed**, -ing, -ation

a The town was totally ______ for the severe flood.

b After careful ______ the group of climbers set out.

8 Two letter clusters have been provided for each word. **Match** them to the words in the box. **Write** the **missing letter cluster** and the **whole word**.

protector fidgeting worshipped decompose specialist leadership

a ist spec ______ ______
b ped ship ______ ______
c tect or ______ ______
d er lead ______ ______
e ing get ______ ______
f pose de ______ ______

9 **Complete** the **synonyms** for the given words by adding the required letters.

a happen oc______
b illness sic______
c awful terr______
d envious jea______
e spoil dam______
f occupy inha______
g amuse ente______
h quickly rapi______

10 **Match** the words in the box to the antonym stems. **Complete** the **antonyms**.

damage punish absent valuable patient kind

a re______
b rew______
c pre______
d worth______
e impat______
f cr______

11 In a dictionary these **key words** are at the top of the pages noted.

enemy (page 59) enrol (page 60) envoy (page 61) equip (page 62)

On **which page** would these words be?

a entry ____
b entice ____
c enrage ____
d engine ____
e epic ____
f essay ____

☞ Answers on page 125

Puzzle time 2

Crossword 2

Across

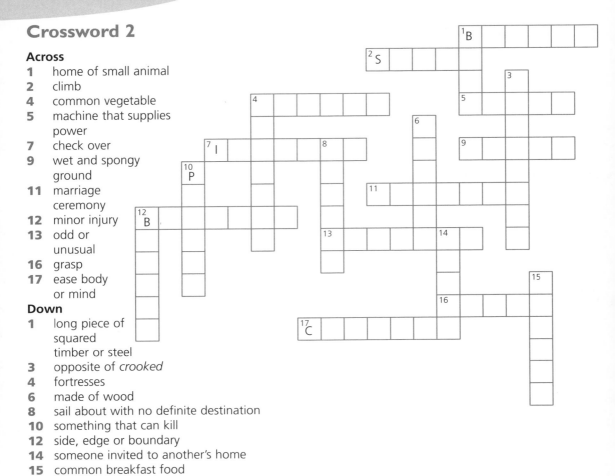

1 home of small animal
2 climb
4 common vegetable
5 machine that supplies power
7 check over
9 wet and spongy ground
11 marriage ceremony
12 minor injury
13 odd or unusual
16 grasp
17 ease body or mind

Down

1 long piece of squared timber or steel
3 opposite of *crooked*
4 fortresses
6 made of wood
8 sail about with no definite destination
10 something that can kill
12 side, edge or boundary
14 someone invited to another's home
15 common breakfast food

Wordsearch 2

There are ten words from Chapter 2 in this word search. They can be horizontal, vertical or diagonal. The words begin with the letters shown in the box on the left.

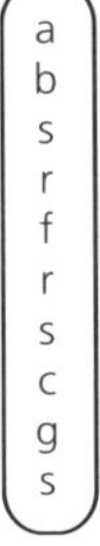

Y Z C M L W H R B X S Y O L M
H Y G R D U I S S O P S B S X
K I G D N I H M T O W E H Q P
B X Q B R T T P E G B Y P Y N
B B K A K S G L A D X R T I R
W O C W B A C R M S E P Y V L
B A L S T Z H H A H G Q G Z A
B R O L T N D P T T U Q L S T
H D S H M W D O R C E U U S M
Q E I S R J M B R A M R I P I
A R N E W S L Q I V P S L Q W
M J G L X U N X N B S P G J F
A W G L N Z O P G A J I E W Y
M H W E N A L N F I N E F D T
T M D R B H U Y E B Q C D R U

Answers on page 125

Spelling rules

- There are a number of **simple rules** that can be applied to many of the words in the English language.
- However, remember that there are **exceptions** to these rules. Knowing the rule will not help you spell these exceptions to the rule. You need to **commit these words to memory**.
- The rules can be divided into several groups related to the following aspects of word study.

Introduction

Parts of speech

Check these definitions of parts of speech you will encounter in Chapters 3–6.

Adjectives

Adjectives are words that describe nouns.

- **Descriptive** adjectives — This is a **huge** building.
- **Numbering** adjectives — Sarah has **seven** new books.
- **Comparing** adjectives — Here is the **smallest** box.
- **Possessive** adjectives — These are **my** clothes.
- **Classifying** adjectives — It is a **Burmese** cat.

Adverbs

Adverbs are words that **describe how**, **when** and **where**. They describe a verb, adjective or another adverb.

She worked **hard**. (how, verb *worked*)

The parcel is **there**. (where, verb *is*)

They walked **quite** slowly. (adverb *slowly*)

Jason will leave **soon**. (when, verb *leave*)

It is a **very** loud sound. (adjective *loud*)

Adverbs can also be used to show different **meanings** or **mood**.

She **often** goes to the shop.

She **seldom** visits her sisters.

Tina could **possibly** go in a few days.

Anya will **probably** return in a week.

Negative adverbs are ***not*** and ***never***.

Nouns

Nouns name people, animals, places, things, feelings and ideas.

- **Proper nouns** are used to **name particular** people, places, events or times and dates:
  Susan *went to* ***Sydney*** *during* ***August*** *for the* ***Allstar Festival****.*
- **Common nouns** are used to **name** any one of a **group** of **things**:
  The ***dog*** *and the* ***cat*** *became good* ***friends*** *last year.*
- **Collective nouns** are used to **name groups** of **things**:
  They saw a ***mob*** *of cattle and a* ***flock*** *of sheep.*
- **Abstract nouns** are used for **thoughts** and **feelings**:
  They gazed in ***wonder*** *at the* ***beauty*** *of the scenery.*

Introduction

Verbs

Verbs are words that **show action**, **feeling**, **thinking**, **saying** or **relating**.

- **Action** She **threw** the ball.
- **Feeling** Sarah **enjoys** playing netball.
- **Thinking** Emma **remembered** the answer.
- **Saying** The coach **shouted** loudly.
- **Relating** The cars **were** bright and shiny.

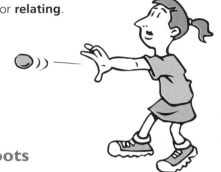

Prefixes, suffixes and Latin and Greek roots

A **prefix** is a word element that, when added to the beginning of a word, **forms** a **new word** (e.g. ***un-*** + *tidy* = *untidy*).

A suffix is a word element that, when added to the end of a word, forms a new word (e.g. *develop* + ***-ment*** = *development*).

A **root** is the **essential part** of a word. It gives its meaning to other words built around it. Many English words have Latin or Greek roots. (These will be studied in Chapter 6.) For example:

- *caput* means head in Latin and so *capital* means the head or main city.
- *ge* means earth in Greek and so *geology* means the study of rocks of the earth.

Many of the prefixes and suffixes used to build words come from Old English, Latin and Greek. For example:

- Old English prefixes ***a-*** ***after-*** ***down-*** ***mis-***
- Latin prefixes ***ante-*** ***circum-*** ***trans-***
- Greek prefixes ***auto-*** ***dia-*** ***hypo-*** ***peri-***
- Old English suffixes ***-er*** ***-hood*** ***-ness*** ***-ship***
- Latin suffixes ***-ant*** ***-ice*** ***-ory*** ***-ate***
- Greek suffixes ***-isk*** ***-ist*** ***-ism***

Language scholars believe that the original English words (of Anglo-Saxon origin) make up about 20 to 30 per cent of the words in modern English.

The English language has absorbed words from many different languages but particularly Latin and Greek. Thousands of words built from Latin or Greek roots were gradually absorbed into the English language during the period from AD 500 to 1500.

Here are some words adapted from those of other countries.

Country	Words
Belgium and Holland	cruise, yacht, smuggle, schooner
France (Normandy)	assault, chivalry, homage, rascal
Spain	castanet, galleon, patio, siesta
Italy	opera, concert, serenade, soprano
America	squaw, moccasin, totem, wigwam

Forming plural nouns – Rules 1–2

In this section, you will learn some useful rules for **forming plural nouns**.

Rule 1

To make a **plural form**, add ***s*** to the singular form. If the noun ends in ***s***, ***x***, ***z***, ***ch*** or ***sh***, add ***es*** to the singular form.

Examples

Adding ***s***	boy ➡ boy**s** wave ➡ wave**s**	girl ➡ girl**s** surprise ➡ surprise**s**	
Adding ***es***	glass ➡ glass**es** peach ➡ peach**es**	tax ➡ tax**es** flash ➡ flash**es**	waltz ➡ waltz**es**

Common exceptions stomach**s** monarch**s**

1 **Write** the **plural form** of each noun below.

kitten cow desk cask branch

fox pen mass quiz leash

2 **Rewrite** the sentences, changing the nouns in **bold** to **plural**. The verbs and articles (*a*/*the*) may also need to be changed to match the plural nouns.

a The **book** and the **glass** were there. ____________

b There was a **patch** on the **dress**. ____________

Rule 2

If a singular noun ends in ***y*** with a consonant before it, make the plural by changing ***y*** to ***i*** and adding ***es***.

The vowels are ***a***, ***e***, ***i***, ***o*** and ***u***. All the other letters are consonants.

Examples

baby ➡ bab**ies** mystery ➡ myster**ies** company ➡ compan**ies** century ➡ centur**ies**
body ➡ bod**ies** industry ➡ industr**ies** family ➡ famil**ies** army ➡ arm**ies**

3 **Write** the **plural form** of the nouns below.

property lorry injury lily gipsy

ruby duty jury gully

4 **Rewrite** the sentences, changing the nouns in **bold** to **plural**. The verbs may need to be changed to match the plural nouns.

a The **lady** was on the **balcony**. ____________

b The **copy** was in the **study**. ____________

☞ Answers on page 126

Forming plural nouns – Rule 3

Rule 3

If a singular noun ends in ***f*** or ***fe***, make the plural by changing the ***f*** or ***fe*** to ***ves***.

Examples

lea**f** ➠ lea**ves**	loa**f** ➠ loa**ves**	wol**f** ➠ wol**ves**	shel**f** ➠ shel**ves**
kni**fe** ➠ kni**ves**	li**fe** ➠ li**ves**	wi**fe** ➠ wi**ves**	thie**f** ➠ thie**ves**

Common exceptions

gul**f** ➠ gul**fs**	relie**f** ➠ relie**fs**	ree**f** ➠ ree**fs**	belie**f** ➠ belie**fs**	brie**f** ➠ brie**fs**
roo**f** ➠ roo**fs**	che**f** ➠ che**fs**	chie**f** ➠ chie**fs**	sa**fe** ➠ sa**fes**	

You can make the plurals of these words by adding ***s*** or by changing ***f*** to ***ves***:

wharf **roof** **scarf** **dwarf** **hoof**

It is your choice.

1 **Write** the **plural form** of these words.

elf	calf	self	wife	half
sheaf	safe	gulf	life	belief

2 **Rewrite** the sentences, changing the nouns in **bold** to **plural**. The verbs may need to be changed to match the plural nouns.

a The **chief** was at the **wharf**. __________

b The **reef** could be seen from the **roof**. __________

Quick check

1 **Write** the **plural form** of these words.

ash	wolf	sound	porch	patch
sky	fairy	monarch	jelly	bus
lion	fox	lass	gully	wallaby
dwarf	church	half	ditch	theory

2 **Rewrite** the sentences, changing the nouns in **bold** to **plural**. The verbs may need to be changed to match the plural nouns.

a The **butterfly** was on the **bush**. __________

b The **injury** was caused by the **knife**. __________

c His **daughter** bought the **box**. __________

d An **adult** went on the **ferry**. __________

Answers on page 126

Forming plural nouns – Rules 4–5

Rule 4

If a singular noun ends in ***y*** with a vowel before the ***y***, make the plural form by simply adding ***s***.

Examples

k**e**y ➟ key**s** | rel**a**y ➟ rela**ys** | kidn**ey** ➟ kidne**ys** | monk**ey** ➟ monke**ys**
all**ey** ➟ alle**ys** | stor**ey** ➟ store**ys** | journ**ey** ➟ journe**ys** | chimn**ey** ➟ chimne**ys**

1 **Write** the **plural form** of these nouns.

display tray railway survey spray buoy essay birthday

____

____

2 **Rewrite** the sentences, changing the **bold** nouns to plural forms. The verbs may need to be changed to match the plural nouns.

a The **jockey** left on his **journey**. ____________________

b The **turkey** roamed into the **valley**. ____________________

Rule 5

If a singular noun ends in ***o***, the plural is usually formed by adding ***es***.

Examples

tomat**o** ➟ tomat**oes** | her**o** ➟ her**oes** | carg**o** ➟ carg**oes**
potat**o** ➟ potat**oes** | volcan**o** ➟ volcan**oes** | ech**o** ➟ ech**oes**

Common exceptions

Some words ending in ***o*** form the plural by adding ***s*** (e.g. pian**o** ➟ pian**os**). Other words are:

kimono | soprano | studio | cello | radio
avocado | fiasco | merino | video | photo

Either ***s*** or ***es*** can be used with these words:

dingo | **halo** | **mosquito** | **grotto** | **buffalo**
zero | **mango** | **motto** | **flamingo** | **ghetto**

It is your choice.

3 **Write** the **plural form** of these nouns.

flamingo domino tornado studio zero torpedo

____

4 **Rewrite** the sentences, changing the **bold** nouns to **plural** forms. The verbs may need to be changed to match the plural nouns.

a The **photo** was in the **studio**. ____________________

b The **echo** was heard beyond the **volcano**. ____________________

c The **mango** was beside the **radio**. ____________________

☞ Answers on page 126

Forming plural nouns – Rule 6

Rule 6

If a singular noun ends in ***ff*** or ***ffe***, make the plural form by adding ***s***.

Examples

cli**ff** ➡ cli**ffs** gira**ffe** ➡ gira**ffes** tari**ff** ➡ tari**ffs** sheri**ff** ➡ sheri**ffs**

1 **Write** the **plural form** of these nouns.

staff cuff bailiff mastiff bluff

2 **Rewrite** the sentences, changing the **bold** nouns to **plural**. The verbs may need to be changed to match the plural nouns.

a The **giraffe** was near the edge of the **cliff**. ______

b The **sheriff** collected the **tariff** at the gate. ______

Quick check

Write the **plural form** of these nouns.

1 chimney echo video cuff storey cello donkey

2 patch lash wax buzz cross half whiff

3 monarch reef safe chef studio soprano reef

Irregular plurals

These plural forms need to be learnt as they do not follow the previous six rules.

- The plurals of **compound words**, including:

  father-in-law ➡ fathers-in-law, son-in-law ➡ sons-in-law, by-way ➡ by-ways, passer-by ➡ passers-by, man-servant ➡ men-servants, man-of-war ➡ men-of-war

- Words that **change internal letters**, including:

  man ➡ men, mouse ➡ mice, woman ➡ women, goose ➡ geese, tooth ➡ teeth, louse ➡ lice, foot ➡ feet

- Words with an **unusual ending** for the plural, including:

  child ➡ children, axis ➡ axes, brother ➡ brethren, terminus ➡ termini, ox ➡ oxen, cactus ➡ cacti, oasis ➡ oases, radius ➡ radii

- Words that have the **same form in singular** and **plural**, including:

  sheep fish deer innings

- Words with **no singular form**, including:

  news species pliers scissors clippers measles tongs glasses (spectacles)

Answers on page 126

Rules 1–6

How much do you know?

1 **Rewrite** these sentences, using the **plural** form of the words in **bold**. Verbs may need to change to match the plural forms.

a The **courier** delivered the crystal **glass** to the **address** on the **box**.

b The **tomato**, **potato** and **avocado** were placed in the crisper **drawer** in the **refrigerator**.

c In the musical **company** the **soprano** also played the **cello** in the **orchestra**.

d The **giraffe**, **buffalo**, **flamingo** and **donkey** visited the **waterhole** regularly.

e The **video** about the **life** of the **wolf** was kept in the fireproof **safe**.

2 **Underline** the **plural forms** that are spelt **incorrectly**. **Write** the **correct form** underneath.

a The echos of the sounds of the erupting volcanos could be heard many kilometres away.

b The mysterys were not solved for many yeares.

c All the monkies in the vallies were making screeching sounds.

d Are the knifes kept on the shelfs near the cupboard?

e The taxs were placed on all the deliverys that had been made.

f All the storys were read by the teachers in the librarys.

g The sandwichs were placed in the studioes for the performers.

h The chimnies are decorated by the wifes of the villagers.

Answers on page 126

Final letter y – Rules 7–9

In this section, you will learn some useful rules for **adding suffixes** to words that **end** in ***y***.

Rule 7

If a noun, adjective or verb ends in ***y*** after a consonant, the ***y*** is changed to ***i*** before adding a suffix -***ful***, -***ness***, -***less***, -***ous***, -***al***, -***ly***, -***ed***, -***er*** or -***est***.

Examples

beaut**y** ➡ beaut**iful** · happ**y** ➡ happ**iness** · merc**y** ➡ merc**iless** · glor**y** ➡ glor**ious**
industr**y** ➡ industr**ial** · bur**y** ➡ bur**ial** · da**y** ➡ da**ily** · certif**y** ➡ certif**ied**
heav**y** ➡ heav**ier** · lonel**y** ➡ lonel**iest**

1 **Add** one of the **suffixes** above to these words.

hungry ____________________ pity ____________________
victory ____________________ certify ____________________
angry ____________________ lazy ____________________

2 **Change** the **bold** words to suit the sentences. **Use** a suitable **suffix**.

a It was the (**silly**) ____________________ movie we had seen.
b The work was done very (**tidy**) ____________________.
c The (**fury**) ____________________ animal charged into the scrub.

Rule 8

If a word ends in ***y*** after a vowel, the ***y*** is not changed before an ending that begins with a vowel.

Examples

ob**ey** ➡ obey**ed** · pl**ay** ➡ play**ed** · j**oy** ➡ joy**ous**

Common exceptions

say ➡ said · pay ➡ paid · lay ➡ laid

Rule 9

If a verb ends in ***y***, the ***y*** is not changed into ***i*** before adding ***ing***.

Examples

hurry ➡ hurrying · marry ➡ marrying · worry ➡ worrying

3 **Write** the ***ing*** form of these verbs.

pity ______________ bury ______________ certify ______________
occupy ______________ tarry ______________ allay ______________

4 **Change** the **bold** words to fit the sentences by **adding** a suitable **ending**.

a They all **enjoy**__________ their day out.
b The goods were **convey**__________ to the front line.
c The **buy**__________ of the material met in the city.

☞ Answers on page 126

Final letter e – Rules 10–11

In this section, you will learn some useful rules for **adding suffixes** to words that **end** in ***e***.

Rule 10

If a word ends in a **silent *e***, the ***e*** is dropped when adding a suffix that begins with a vowel: ***-ous***, ***-able***, ***-ible***, ***-ical***, ***-ing***, ***-ion***.

Examples

liv**e** ➡ liv**ing**   continu**e** ➡ continu**ous**   excit**e** ➡ excit**able**

Common exceptions

se**e** ➡ se**eing**   agre**e** ➡ agre**eable**   chang**e** ➡ chang**eable**

1 **Add** one of the **suffixes** above to these words.

quote ____________   measure ____________
cone ____________   come ____________
graze ____________   insinuate ____________

2 **Change** the **bold** words to fit the sentences by **adding** a suitable **suffix**.

a The small animal was a (**like**) ____________ creature.
b They attended the (**graduate**) ____________ ceremony.
c The (**glaze**) ____________ replaced the broken window pane.

Rule 11

If a word ends in a **silent *e***, the ***e*** is kept before a syllable or suffix beginning with a consonant: ***-ly***, ***-ful***, ***-ment***, ***-ty***, ***-ness***.

Examples

wis**e** ➡ wis**ely**   lov**e** ➡ lov**ely**   nin**e** ➡ nin**ety**

Common exceptions

wis**e** ➡ wis**dom**   whol**e** ➡ whol**ly**   tru**e** ➡ tru**ly**   judg**e** ➡ judg**ment**

3 **Add** a **syllable** or **suffix** beginning with a consonant to these words.

use ____________   move ____________
same ____________   place ____________
shame ____________   shape ____________

4 **Change** the **bold** words to fit the sentences by **adding** a suitable **ending**.

a They travelled in **safe**________ across the mountains.
b It was a very **tune**________ sound.
c The design, which had been used for many years, was regarded as an **age**________ design.

☞ Answers on page 126

Rules 7–11

1 **Identify** the number of the **rule** each pair of words illustrates. Check back to the previous pages if necessary.

a carr**y** — carr**ying** ___

b displac**e** — displac**ement** ___

c graz**e** — graz**ier** ___

d victor**y** — victor**ious** ___

2 Is the spelling of the **second word** in each pair **correct**? **Tick** (✓) the yes or no box. If no, **write** the word **correctly**. Indicate the **rule number**.

a nerve — nerveous Yes ❑ No ❑ ________________ Rule ___

b carry — carring Yes ❑ No ❑ ________________ Rule ___

c office — official Yes ❑ No ❑ ________________ Rule ___

d lonely — loneliness Yes ❑ No ❑ ________________ Rule ___

e prince — princly Yes ❑ No ❑ ________________ Rule ___

f pity — pityless Yes ❑ No ❑ ________________ Rule ___

3 Use the exceptions to the rules given in the box to complete the following sentences.

say — said	pay — paid	lay — laid	true — truly
see — seeing	agree — agreeable	change — changeable	
wise — wisdom	whole — wholly	judge — judgement	

a The goods were ______________________ for by my brother.

b She is the most ______________________ girl I know.

c I do not like this ______________________ weather.

d The veteran climber spoke with great ______________________.

e She was ______________________ responsible for making the mistake.

4 **Change** the **bold** words to fit the sentences by **adding** a suitable **suffix** or **ending**.

a They performed a very (**grace**) __________________________ dance.

b Because of his (**lazy**) __________________________ the work was not completed.

c It was the (**fine**) __________________________ of all the products on display.

d They were all (**qualify**) __________________________ to repair the pumps.

e The mice were (**scamper**) __________________________ across the floor.

f It was broken because it had been (**misuse**) __________________________.

☞ Answers on pages 126–127

Final consonants – Rules 12–14

In this section, you will learn some useful rules for **adding suffixes** to words that **end** in a **consonant**.

Rule 12

If a **one syllable word** ends in a **consonant preceded by only one vowel**, **double** the **last letter** when adding an ending that begins with a vowel.

Examples

dr**op** ➡ dro**pp**ed   r**un** ➡ ru**nn**ing   h**ot** ➡ ho**tt**er   b**it** ➡ bi**tt**en   w**in** ➡ wi**nn**er
d**ig** ➡ di**gg**ing   c**an** ➡ ca**nn**ing   fl**og** ➡ flo**gg**ed   sw**im** ➡ swi**mm**er

1 **Add** an **ending** or **suffix** to these words.

beg ______________   rid ______________   thin ______________
big ______________   trip ______________   let ______________

2 **Change** the **bold** words to fit the sentences by **adding** a suitable **ending**.

a The water from the valley was (**dam**) ____________________ up for a distance of three kilometres.
b The poachers had (**drug**) ____________________ the animal's water supply.
c The (**wed**) ____________________ was held last Saturday.

Rule 13

If a word of **more than one syllable** (with the **accent** on the **last syllable**) ends in a **consonant preceded by one vowel**, **double** the **last letter** when adding an ending that begins with a vowel.

Accent is the **stress** or stronger tone given to part of a word (e.g. *accident* has the accent on ***acc*** and *admire* has the accent on ***mire***).

Examples

perm**it** ➡ permi**tt**ing   ref**er** ➡ refe**rr**ing   forg**ot** ➡ forgo**tt**en   occ**ur** ➡ occu**rr**ed

Rule 14

If a word ends in ***l***, always **double** the ***l*** before adding a suffix beginning with a vowel.

Examples

quarre**l** ➡ quarre**ll**ed   cance**l** ➡ cance**ll**ed

3 **Add** an **ending** or **suffix** to these words.

admit ______________________________   regret ______________________________
compel ______________________________   cruel ______________________________

4 **Change** the **bold** words to fit the sentences by **adding** a **suitable ending**.

a The girl (**prefer**) ______________________________ to continue with her lesson.
b All the land had been (**allot**) ______________________________ to the newcomers.
c At the (**begin**) ______________________________ of the day the fencers moved in.

Answers on page 127

Final consonants – Rules 15–16

Rule 15

If a word ends in a **consonant preceded by another consonant** or by **more than one vowel**, the last letter is **not doubled** when adding a syllable or suffix beginning with a vowel.

Examples

sw**eet** ➡ sw**eeten** b**oil** ➡ b**oiling** w**ait** ➡ w**aiter** **eat** ➡ **eating**
ch**eap** ➡ ch**eaper** w**ood** ➡ w**ooden**

Common exceptions wool ➡ woollen

1 **Add** a suitable **ending** or **suffix** to these words.

leap ______________ lean ______________
toil ______________ teem ______________
droop ______________ land ______________

2 **Change** the **bold** word to fit the sentence by **adding** a suitable **ending**.

a The special (**link**) ______________ on the tractor had broken away.
b It was the (**mild**) ______________ soap I have ever used.
c The (**paint**) ______________ had completed the work early.

Rule 16

If a word of **more than one syllable** (with the **last syllable not accented**) ends in a consonant, the last letter is **not doubled** when adding a suffix beginning with a vowel.

Examples

happe**n** ➡ happe**ned** visi**t** ➡ visi**tor** prefe**r** ➡ prefe**rence**

Common exceptions

handicap ➡ handicapped kidnap ➡ kidnapped worship ➡ worshipped

3 **Add** a suitable **ending** or **suffix** to these words.

border ______________ benefit ______________
murmur ______________ wander ______________

4 **Change** the word in **bold** to fit the sentence by **adding** a suitable **ending**.

a The wrestler (**shoulder**) ______________ his opponent into the ropes.

b She (**whisper**) ______________ quietly to her neighbour.

c The traveller had been (**wander**) ______________ in many lands.

Answers on page 127

Rules 12–16

1. **Identify** the **number of the rule** illustrated by these pairs of words. Check back to the preceding pages if necessary.

   a spot — spotted ___ **b** prohibit — prohibitive ___
   c forgot — forgotten ___ **d** spoil — spoiling ___

2. Is the spelling of the **second word** in each pair **correct**? **Tick** (✓) the yes or no box. If no, **write** the word **correctly**. Indicate the **rule number**.

   a predict — predicttable Yes ☐ No ☐ ______________ Rule ___
   b project — projectted Yes ☐ No ☐ ______________ Rule ___
   c leap — leapping Yes ☐ No ☐ ______________ Rule ___
   d cancel — cancelling Yes ☐ No ☐ ______________ Rule ___
   e set — seting Yes ☐ No ☐ ______________ Rule ___
   f mob — mobbed Yes ☐ No ☐ ______________ Rule ___

3. **Use** the words in the box (exceptions to the rules in this section) to **complete** the following **sentences**.

wool — woollen	handicap — handicapped
kidnap — kidnapped	worship — worshipped

   a The beautiful ______________ coat kept out the cold winds.
   b The child was ______________ by unknown criminals.
   c The people ______________ at the shrine.
   d The travellers were ______________ by the heavy load and took many hours to complete the journey.

4. **Change** the **bold** word to fit the sentence by **adding** a suitable **suffix** or **ending**.

   a The money was **conceal** under the old sacks.
   ____
   b At the **begin** of the day they set out.
   ____
   c The way was **bar** by a large landslide.
   ____
   d She **grin** at the antics of the clown.
   ____
   e The plan was **reject** by the member of the council.
   ____
   f The enemy forces were **repel** by our troops.
   ____

☞ Answers on page 127

Prefixes and suffixes – Rules 17–20

In this section, you will learn some useful rules for **adding prefixes** and **suffixes**.

Rule 17

If -***full*** is used as a **suffix**, one ***l*** is dropped.

Examples

use + fu**ll** = usefu**l** doubt + fu**ll** = doubtfu**l**

1 **Add** the suffix -***full*** (meaning *full of*) to these words.

hand ____________ harm ____________ faith ____________

wonder ____________ spoon ____________ cheer ____________

Rule 18

If the prefix ***dis***- or ***mis***- is added to a word, **never drop** the ***s*** (even if the original word begins with ***s***).

Examples

dis + agree = di**s**agree
dis + **s**atisfy = di**ss**atisfy

mis + inform = mi**s**inform
mis + **s**pell = mi**ss**pell

2 **Add** the prefix ***dis***- (meaning *away* or *apart*) to these words.

locate ____________ place ____________

3 **Add** the prefix ***mis***- (meaning *wrong*) to these words.

count ____________ judge ____________

Rule 19

If ***able*** or ***ous*** is added to a word ending in ***ce*** or ***ge***, **do not drop** the final ***e***.

Examples

chan**ge** + **able** = chang**eable** coura**ge** + **ous** = coura**geous**

Common exception

practi**ce** + **able** = practi**cable**

4 **Add** the suffixes -***able*** (meaning *capable of*) or -***ous*** to these words.

advantage ____________ manage ____________

peace ____________ service ____________

Rule 20

If the suffix -***ness*** is added to a word that **already ends in *n***, the ending becomes ***nness***.

Examples

sudde**n** + **ness** = sudde**nness** kee**n** + **ness** = kee**nness**

5 **Add** the suffix -***ness*** (meaning *state of being*) to these words.

mean ____________ stubborn ____________

lean ____________ even ____________

☞ Answers on page 127

Adjectives and adverbs – Rules 21–23

In this section, you will learn some useful rules for **forming adverbs** from **adjectives**.

Rule 21

If an **adjective ends** in ***le***, the ***e*** is **dropped** and ***y*** is **added** to form the adverb.

Examples

sing**le** ➡ sing**ly** idl**e** ➡ id**ly** suitab**le** ➡ suitab**ly**

1 **Change** these adjectives to **adverbs**.

noble ____________ probable ____________

notable ____________ agreeable ____________

Rule 22

If ***ly*** is added to an adjective that already ends in ***l***, the adverb ends in ***lly***.

Examples

usua**l** ➡ usua**lly** faithfu**l** ➡ faithfu**lly**

2 **Add *ly*** to these adjectives to form adverbs.

real ____________ general ____________

natural ____________ joyful ____________

equal ____________ final ____________

Rule 23

If a word ends in ***our***, the ***u*** is **often dropped** when a **suffix beginning** with a **vowel** is added.

Examples

hum**our** ➡ hum**orous** rig**our** ➡ rig**orous**

Common exceptions

hon**our** ➡ hon**ourable** fav**our** ➡ fav**ourable**

3 **Add** a **suffix ending** with a **vowel** to these words.

vigour ____________ vapour ____________

Answers on page 127

Other rules – Rules 24–27

Rule 24

If a word has the letters ***e*** and ***i*** making the **ee** sound, the ***i*** comes before ***e*** except after ***c***.

Examples rel**ie**ve y**ie**ld f**ie**ld bel**ie**ve rec**ei**ve dec**ei**ve

Common exception seize

1 **Insert** the letters ***ie*** or ***ei*** into the following words.

sh____ld n____ce ach____ve d____sel perc____ve

Rule 25

The letter ***c*** is used for **nouns** while ***s*** is used for **verbs**.

Examples practi**c**e (noun) — practi**s**e (verb) devi**c**e (noun) — devi**s**e (verb)

Common exception promise (noun and verb)

2 **Insert** the letter ***c*** or ***s*** into the words in **bold** in these sentences.

a She had lost her driver's **licen___e**.

b The government department will **licen___e** the builder's work on the site.

c The **prophe___y** of the village elder eventually came true.

Rule 26

Verbs that end in ***ie*** change ***ie*** to ***y*** before adding ***ing***.

Examples die ➡ dying lie ➡ lying tie ➡ tying

Rule 27

The letter ***q*** is always **followed** by ***u***.

Examples **qu**estion **qu**arrel e**qu**al re**qu**ire **qu**ality **qu**arter con**qu**er **qu**ick **qu**antity

Silent letters

Silent letters are letters that you **do not sound** when the word is said. Note the silent letters in the following words.

b lam**b** bom**b** thum**b** lim**b** num**b** de**b**t dou**b**t com**b** plum**b**er

c s**c**ene mus**c**le ya**c**ht

g forei**g**n si**g**n desi**g**n campai**g**n resi**g**n **g**naw **g**nat soverei**g**n

h **h**onour **h**onest **h**eir **h**our ve**h**icle

k **k**not **k**nit **k**nife **k**now **k**nee

l ha**l**f ca**l**f cha**l**k ca**l**m pa**l**m wou**l**d sa**l**mon cou**l**d shou**l**d

n autum**n** colum**n** solem**n** hym**n**

p **p**salm cor**p**s **p**neumonia

s i**s**land ai**s**le i**s**le

t lis**t**en fas**t**en cas**t**le whis**t**le wres**t**le balle**t**

w **w**rong **w**rite **w**rap **w**rist **w**reck ans**w**er s**w**ord

☞ Answers on page 127

Rules 17–27

1 **Add** the **suffix** meaning *full of* to these words.

a power ______ b success ______
c thought ______ d truth ______

2 **Add** the **prefix** ***dis*** or ***mis*** to these words.

a approve ______ b calculate ______
c deed ______ d appoint ______
e apply ______ f close ______

3 Is the spelling of the **second word** in each pair **correct**? **Tick** (P) the yes or no box. If no, **write** the word **correctly**. Indicate the **rule number**.

a suitable — suitablely Yes ☐ No ☐ ______ Rule ___
b green — greenness Yes ☐ No ☐ ______ Rule ___
c manage — managable Yes ☐ No ☐ ______ Rule ___
d courage — courageous Yes ☐ No ☐ ______ Rule ___
e eventual — eventualy Yes ☐ No ☐ ______ Rule ___
f faithful — faithfuly Yes ☐ No ☐ ______ Rule ___

4 **Use** the exceptions to the rules in the box to **complete** the following **sentences**.

practice — practicable honour — honourable favour — favourable seize

a The officer received an ______ discharge from the armed forces.
b It was not ______ for the huge dam to be built within two years.
c The team will ______ the rope and lift the heavy weight.
d The company was provided with a ______ report on the work of the employee.

5 **Circle** the **silent letters** in the following words.

a pseudonym b gnash
c knight d knob
e gnome f writer
g psychology h glisten
i consign j baulk
k wreckage l knoll

6 **Add** ***ing*** to the words in **bold** to **complete** these sentences.

a The animal was (**die**) ______ by the side of the road.
b The girl was (**lie**) ______ on the couch in the sick room.
c They were (**tie**) ______ up the bundles of straw.

☞ Answers on page 127

Review test 3

1 **Rewrite** the sentences using the **plural** form of the words in **bold**.

a The **ferry** rounded the **buoy** at the **entrance** to the bay.

____

____

b The **echo** of the **sound** could be heard in the **valley**.

____

____

c His **brother-in-law** took the **cargo** to the **terminus**.

____

____

d Their **nephew** and his **wife** learnt the **melody**.

____

____

2 **Underline** any **incorrect plural** forms. **Write** the **correct plurals** underneath.

a The dairys were owned by familys in many countrys.

____

b There were flashs of light on the glasss in the cupboards.

____

c All their lifes the turkies had lived in the gullys.

____

3 **Write** the **plural** form of these words.

photo	________	radio	________
volcano	________	mastiff	________
display	________	monarch	________
man	________	by-way	________
oasis	________	child	________
ox	________	tooth	________

4 **Identify** the **number of the rule** illustrated by these pairs of words. Check back over the chapter if necessary.

a	ferry — ferrying	Rule ___	b	glory — glorify	Rule ___
c	trip — tripped	Rule ___	d	omit — omitting	Rule ___
e	replace — replacement	Rule ___	f	nice — nicely	Rule ___
g	model — modelling	Rule ___	h	steep — steepest	Rule ___

☞ Answers on page 127

Review test 3

5 Is the spelling of the **second word** in each pair **correct**? **Tick** (✓) the yes or no box. If no, **write** the word **correctly**. Indicate the **rule number**.

a	waltz — waltzs	Yes ☐	No ☐	____________	Rule __
b	lonely — lonelyier	Yes ☐	No ☐	____________	Rule __
c	tag — taging	Yes ☐	No ☐	____________	Rule __
d	century — centurys	Yes ☐	No ☐	____________	Rule __
e	visit — visittor	Yes ☐	No ☐	____________	Rule __
f	fine — finly	Yes ☐	No ☐	____________	Rule __
g	monkey — monkeys	Yes ☐	No ☐	____________	Rule __
h	scurry — scurrying	Yes ☐	No ☐	____________	Rule __
i	gulf — gulfes	Yes ☐	No ☐	____________	Rule __
j	tomato — tomatos	Yes ☐	No ☐	____________	Rule __

6 **Underline** the words **spelt incorrectly**. **Write** them correctly.

a They layd the bricks on the beautiful driveway.

____

b All the children enjoyed what the visitor sayd.

____

c She had been liveing there and often plaied in the park.

____

d Were the knifes left near the scissores?

____

e The heavyer parcels were droped into the back of the vehicle.

____

7 **Tick** (✓) the words that are correct. **Write** the incorrect words in correct form.

a	injuries	____________	**b**	chefs	____________
c	pianos	____________	**d**	certifyed	____________
e	shadyest	____________	**f**	displays	____________
g	tuneful	____________	**h**	cheapest	____________
i	paid	____________	**j**	potatoes	____________
k	furyious	____________	**l**	wagging	____________
m	lovly	____________	**n**	bluffes	____________
o	forgoten	____________	**p**	visittor	____________

☞ Answers on pages 127–128

Puzzle time 3

Crossword 3

Across

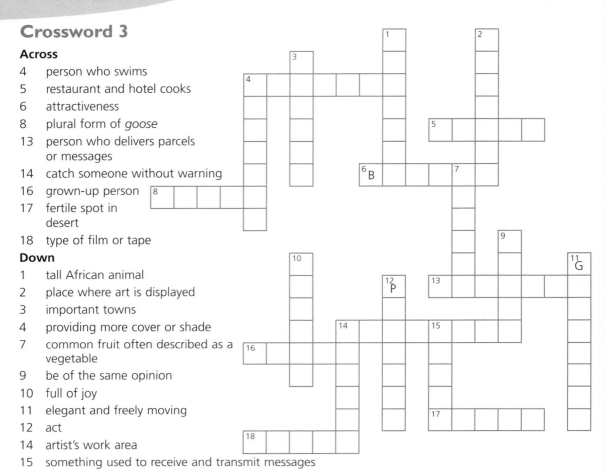

4 person who swims
5 restaurant and hotel cooks
6 attractiveness
8 plural form of *goose*
13 person who delivers parcels or messages
14 catch someone without warning
16 grown-up person
17 fertile spot in desert
18 type of film or tape

Down

1 tall African animal
2 place where art is displayed
3 important towns
4 providing more cover or shade
7 common fruit often described as a vegetable
9 be of the same opinion
10 full of joy
11 elegant and freely moving
12 act
14 artist's work area
15 something used to receive and transmit messages

Wordsearch 3

There are ten words from Chapter 3 in this word search. They can be horizontal, vertical or diagonal. The words begin with the letters shown in the box on the left.

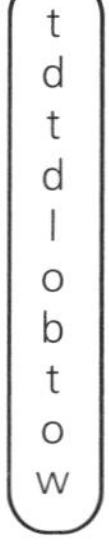

V	K	I	B	Z	S	B	T	L	V	T	T	J	N	T
C	A	J	B	B	Y	M	F	F	E	L	E	G	V	C
T	C	O	T	T	V	E	P	M	I	N	Y	E	J	D
H	D	Z	A	S	E	A	D	Q	U	O	B	C	T	J
I	W	F	B	S	E	T	E	S	F	U	R	J	O	H
E	X	Q	D	L	E	L	L	O	C	C	U	P	Y	Q
V	B	R	I	X	B	S	I	K	Y	C	F	L	T	F
E	E	B	S	T	O	O	V	H	O	N	N	U	F	W
S	Y	S	P	L	W	Z	E	C	I	W	V	Z	G	D
J	E	W	L	Z	W	I	R	Y	E	U	I	H	F	F
W	K	M	A	C	B	Q	I	C	O	F	T	S	O	Q
M	Z	J	Y	R	R	B	E	N	D	G	L	R	E	A
B	N	Z	X	G	A	Q	S	L	Y	Q	L	E	U	Z
N	E	A	J	G	B	U	T	T	E	R	F	L	Y	E
U	L	X	U	S	X	M	B	F	M	X	R	F	C	A

Answers on page 128

4 Word builders: prefixes

In this chapter, you will practise **building words** using **prefixes**.

- Prefixes are **word builders**.
- A prefix is a single letter or syllable added to the **beginning** of a word.
- Most prefixes in common use come from **Latin** and **Greek words**.

Prefixes meaning *against or from*

In this section, you will practise using **prefixes** that mean **against** or **from**.

Prefix	Example
with-	**with**hold = hold **from** or **against**
anti- **ant**-	**anti**dote = medicine that works **against** a poison
contra-	**contra**dict = state something **against** another statement
ob- **op**-	**ob**ject = complain **against**

Word bank

with-	**with**stand **with**draw
anti- **ant**-	**anti**septic **anti**pathy **ant**agonist **Ant**arctic **ant**onym
contra-	**contra**ry **contra**st **contra**band **contra**vene
ob- **op**-	**ob**stacle **ob**struct **op**ponent **op**press

1 **Which words** from the word bank **match** these meanings?

a feeling against something or someone ____________________

b goods moved against the law ____________________

c one who is against you in sport or competition ____________________

d opposite or against something ____________________

e go against or infringe a rule or law ____________________

2 **Choose** suitable words from the word bank to **complete** the following sentences.

a The strongly constructed building was able to ____________________ the strong winds.

b She used the ____________________ ointment to help heal the wound.

c No polar bears live in the ____________________ region.

d The use of ____________________ in the painting made it a very attractive work.

e Did this ____________________ in the road cause the accident?

3 **Add** suitable **endings** to the words in **bold** to complete these sentences.

a My sister was **withdraw**________ money from the ATM.

b His **antagon**________ towards his brother was quite clear.

c Because of the leaders' **contraven**________ of international law, a group of United Nations officials visited the country.

d The **oppress**________ of the people had continued for centuries.

Answers on page 128

Prefixes meaning *above, over, under or beneath*

In this section, you will practise using **prefixes** that mean **above**, **over**, **under** or **beneath**.

Prefix	Example
over-	**over**coat = a coat put on **over** other clothing
super- **sur-**	**super**vise = to look **over** others' work
hypo-	**hypo**dermic = instrument to inject fluids **beneath** the skin
under-	**under**pay = to pay **under** the normal amount
sub- **suf-** **sub-** **sus-**	**sub**marine = vessel that travels **beneath** the ocean

Word bank

over-	**over**charge **over**flow **over**hang **over**head **over**throw
super- **sur-**	**super**visor **super**structure **sur**face **sur**vey **sur**pass
hypo-	**hypo**crite **hypo**thesis
under-	**under**mine **under**weight **under**world **under**ground
sub- **suf-** **sup-** **sus-**	**sub**merge **sub**mit **sub**way **sub**-inspector **suf**fer **sup**port **sup**press **sus**pend **sus**tain

1 **Which words** from the word bank above **match** these meanings?

- **a** to flow over or above the normal amount ______________________
- **b** parts of a ship above the main deck ______________________
- **c** the idea beneath a research finding ______________________
- **d** the criminal element beneath normal society ______________________
- **e** to press news or information under or out of the way ______________________

2 **Choose** suitable **words** from the word bank to **complete** these sentences.

- **a** The helicopter flew directly ______________________ in pursuit of the escapees.
- **b** The ______________________ of the whole project was very pleased with the results.
- **c** The scientist had great difficulty proving that his original ______________________ was correct.
- **d** Because of the drought many of the calves were ______________________.
- **e** Did the architect ______________________ the plans for approval?
- **f** There was not enough food in the village to ______________________ human life.
- **g** The court will ______________________ the driver's licence for six months.

3 **Add** suitable **endings** to the words in **bold** to complete these sentences.

- **a** The **survey**________ was able to work out the best position for the new road.
- **b** Many of the children **suffer**________ from common illnesses.
- **c** The **supervis**________ of the project was very thorough.

☞ Answers on page 128

Prefixes meaning *before, after or between*

In this section, you will practise using **prefixes** that mean **before**, **after** or **between**.

Prefix	Example
fore-	**fore**noon = the time **before** noon
ante-	**ante**room = a room **before** the main room
pre-	**pre**fix = a letter or syllable **before** the main part of the word
pro-	**pro**phet = one who tells of happenings **before** they occur
post-	**post**pone = to put off until **after** the normal date
inter-	**inter**state = happening **between** two or more states

Word bank

fore-/for-	**fore**see **fore**tell **for**ward **fore**head
ante-/anti-	**ante**chamber **anti**cipate **ante**cedent
pre-	**pre**cede **pre**dict **pre**pare **pre**vent
pro-	**pro**gramme **pro**logue **pro**phecy
post-	**post**script **post** mortem **post**date
inter-	**inter**cept **inter**cede **inter**mix **inter**weave **inter**fere

1 **Which words** from the word bank above **match** these meanings?

- **a** to tell or explain something before it occurs ________________
- **b** to realise something before it actually happens ________________
- **c** to go before others in a group or individually ________________
- **d** verses recited before or as the first part of a play ________________
- **e** something written after the main body of a letter ________________
- **f** to meddle with matters between persons ________________

2 **Choose** suitable **words** from the word bank to **complete** these sentences.

- **a** The sailors could not ________________ the dangers ahead of them.
- **b** The child was asked to find the ________________ of the relative pronoun.
- **c** Was it possible to ________________ the ship capsizing in the harbour?
- **d** The people of the village found that the ancient ________________ came true.
- **e** The ________________ on the man who died at the weekend will take place today.
- **f** The skilful player will ________________ the pass and score the winning try.

3 **Add** suitable **endings** to the words in **bold** to complete these sentences.

- **a** All the **prepar**________ were made for the great event.
- **b** The children looked forward with great **anticipa**________ to the festival

Answers on page 128

Prefixes meaning *down*, *away*, *beyond* or *beside*

In this section, you will practise using **prefixes** that mean **down**, **away**, **beyond** or **beside**.

Prefix	Example
de-	**de**scend = to go or climb **down**
cata-	**cata**comb = caves or galleries **down** below the earth's surface
a-, ab-	**ab**sent = to be **away** from a particular place
dis-, di-	**di**vert = to turn **away** from
extra-	**extra**ordinary = **beyond** the ordinary
out-	**out**cast = one who is cast **beyond** a place
para-	**para**ble = story with a message **beside** it or included

CATACOMBS

Word bank

de-	**de**part **de**crease **de**flect **de**celerate
cata-	**cata**logue **cata**pult **cata**strophe
a- ab-	**a**vert **ab**breviate **ab**normal **ab**stract
dis- di-	**dis**locate **dis**pel **dis**sect **dis**solve **dis**tract
extra-	**extra**dite **extra**neous **extra**vagant
out-	**out**live **out**last **out**run **out**stretch **out**law
para-	**para**llel **para**graph **para**pet **para**site

1 **Which words** from the word bank above **match** these meanings?

- **a** to slow down either as an individual or vehicle ______________
- **b** something that throws objects down or away ______________
- **c** away from the normal ______________
- **d** to draw attention away from something ______________
- **e** material or information beyond what is needed ______________
- **f** one who lives beyond the law ______________
- **g** low wall at the edge of a roof ______________

2 **Choose** suitable **words** from the word bank to **complete** these sentences.

- **a** The student drew two sets of ______________ lines on the chart.
- **b** Sally will ______________ her sister in the long distance event.
- **c** The police hoped to ______________ the suspect to answer the charges.
- **d** The scientists will ______________ the body of the dead creature.
- **e** The tsunami was a great ______________.
- **f** The amount he owes will ______________ each year as the debt is paid off.
- **g** All the items for sale were written down in the ______________.

☞ Answers on page 128

Prefixes

1 **Join** the **prefixes** in the circle to the **word stems** in the box. **Write** the **words**.

with dis
over sub de
ob under fore
super out

cut	struction	
arm	drew	array
tain	side	grown
human	rank	

______________________ ______________________
______________________ ______________________
______________________ ______________________
______________________ ______________________
______________________ ______________________

2 **Build** a word from the **prefix** shown in **bold** to **complete** the **sentence**.

a The fire fighters found it difficult to **with**__________ the heat from the fire.
b His **ant**__________ in the contest was a very skilful wrestler.
c The players were standing at **op**__________ ends of the court.
d It is a serious offence to bring in **contra**__________ drugs or other substances.

3 **Change** the words by **adding** one of these **endings**: ***-ion***, ***-y***, ***-ed***. **Write** the new words.

a distract __________ b decelerate __________
c supervisor __________ d extract __________
e anticipate __________ f overflow __________
g intercept __________ h predict __________

4 **Underline** the **prefix**. **Write** the **meaning** of the prefix.

a parallelogram __________
b disappear __________
c abstain __________
d outpost __________
e cataract __________
f detach __________

5 **Draw** a **line** from the **word** to its **matching meaning**.

a intermix — avoid beforehand
b dislocate — turn something away
c avert — place or locate away
d prevent — mix between

Answers on pages 128–129

Prefixes meaning *to, into, across* or *through*

In this section, you will practise using **prefixes** that mean **to**, **into**, **across** or **through**.

Prefix	Example
ad-	**ad**dition = something added **to**
ac-	**ac**cept = to take **to** oneself
ar-	**ar**rive = to get to
at-	**at**tempt = to try **to**
in- **im**-	**in**clude = to shut **into**; **im**port = to bring **into**
trans-	**trans**port = to carry **across**
per-	**per**sist = to work **through** thoroughly
dia-	**dia**gonal = a line **through** a plane surface

Word bank

ad- **ac**-	**ad**here **ad**verb **ad**jacent **ac**cess **ac**claim
ar- **at**-	**ar**rest **ar**range **at**tract **at**tach
in- **im**-	**in**vade **in**sight **im**pose **im**migrate
trans-	**trans**late **trans**fer **trans**cribe **trans**mit
per-	**per**spire **per**form **per**ennial
dia-	**dia**meter **dia**logue **dia**lect

1 **Which words** from the word bank above **match** these meanings?

a to be in a position next to another ____________

b to draw someone's attention to something ____________

c to come from one country into another ____________

d to last through the whole year ____________

e the lines spoken through a play ____________

f to send a message across an area ____________

2 **Choose** suitable **words** from the word bank to **complete** these **sentences**.

a The adults were not given ____________ to the highly confidential documents.

b This small creature will ____________ itself to a much larger fish.

c The army group began to ____________ the territory to the east.

d It was her task to ____________ the information into another language.

e The runners began to ____________ heavily in the humid conditions.

f Each of the regions spoke a different ____________ developed over hundreds of years.

3 **Add** suitable **endings** to the words in **bold** to **complete** these **sentences**.

a The **attract**________ painting was on display yesterday.

b The department handling the **immigrat**________ of new settlers will approve the application.

c The **perform**________ of the singer was outstanding.

Answers on page 129

Prefixes meaning *out of, upwards, middle or upon*

In this section, you will practise using **prefixes** that mean **out of**, **upwards**, **middle** or **upon**.

Prefix	Example
e- ex-	**e**ject = to throw **out of**; **ex**port = to carry **out of**
up-	**up**lands = the land found **upwards** from the plain
mid-	**mid**day = the **middle** of the day
epi-	**epi**taph = words written **upon** a tombstone

Word bank

e- ex-	**e**ducate **e**migrate **ex**ceed **ex**claim **ex**pel
up-	**up**hill **up**hold **up**set **up**right **up**lift
mid-	**mid**air **mid**night **mid**week **mid**summer **mid**ocean
epi-	**epi**demic **epi**logue **epi**centre

1 **Which words** from the word bank above **match** these meanings?

a to go out of or beyond a limit ________________

b to lift in an upward direction ________________

c middle of the hottest months of the year ________________

d serious illness falling upon a population ________________

e the area upon which an earthquake is centred ________________

f to lead out of ignorance ________________

g a speech upon the end of a play ________________

2 **Choose** suitable **words** from the word bank to **complete** these **sentences**.

a The school will ________________ those students for their bad behaviour.

b The machine had to be kept in an ________________ position for it to work correctly.

c The yacht was caught in the ________________ currents for several days.

d During the early part of the twentieth century there was a serious ____________, which killed many people.

e The family decided to ________________ from the small island.

3 **Add** suitable **endings** to the words in **bold** to **complete** these **sentences**.

a The **educat**________ department had set out a new course of study.

b The news was very **upset**________ for the whole family.

c All the poisonous gases were **expel**________ from the small room.

☞ Answers on page 129

Prefixes meaning *with*, *together*, *back* or *again*

In this section, you will practise using **prefixes** that mean **with**, **together**, **back** or **again**.

Prefix	Example
con-	**con**nect = to join **together**
co-	**co**operate = to work **together**
com-	**com**pare = to put **together**
syn-	**syn**onym = a word **with** the same meaning as another
sym-	**sym**pathy = feeling **with** another
re-	**re**join = to join **back** or **again**

Word bank

con- co-	**con**fer **con**flict **con**struct **con**cur **co**incide **con**ference
com-	**com**bat **com**plete **com**pare **com**mune
syn-	**syn**od **syn**opsis **syn**thesis **syn**dicate
sym-	**sym**metry **sym**phony **sym**bol
re-	**re**cite **re**cline **re**cur **re**fer **re**pay

1 **Which words** from the word bank above **match** these meanings?

a to build with or together ____________

b a place where people live and work together ____________

c a group of people working or investing together ____________

d relationship of two parts with the same proportions ____________

e harmonious sounds of instruments together ____________

f to happen again ____________

2 **Choose** suitable **words** from the word bank to **complete** these **sentences**.

a All the top salespeople attended the ____________ at the Gold Coast.

b The scientists will ____________ the two sets of results.

c The ____________ won a major prize in the contest.

d Here is the ____________ that stands for nitrogen.

e The bank will ____________ the matter to the police for action.

3 **Add** suitable **endings** to the words in **bold** to **complete** these **sentences**.

a It was a **coincid**________ that we met our friends at the show.

b The diamond shaped rug is **symmetri**________ in shape.

c The **repay**________ was made some time ago.

Answers on page 129

Prefixes meaning *not, the opposite of, round or about*

In this section, you will practise using **prefixes** that mean **not**, **the opposite of**, **round** or **about**.

Prefix	Example
un-	**un**clean = not or **the opposite of** clean
n- non-	**n**ever = **not** ever; **non**sense = **not** sense
in-	**in**sincere = **not** sincere
il-	**il**legal = **not** legal
im-	**im**possible = **not** possible
ir-	**ir**regular = **not** regular
circum-	**circum**ference = the distance **round** a circle
peri-	**peri**meter = the distance **round** a shape

Word bank

un-	**un**healthy **un**common **un**fold **un**happy **un**lock
n- non-	**n**either **n**one **non**human **non**-event
in- il-	**in**curable **in**animate **in**visible **il**legal
im- ir-	**im**mortal **im**pure **ir**religious **ir**resistible
circum-	**circum**navigate **circum**spect **circum**vent
peri-	**peri**scope **peri**odic **peri**phery

1 **Which words** from the word bank above **match** these meanings?

a not or the opposite of ordinary or common ____________

b a happening or event that is of no value ____________

c not living or breathing ____________

d not able to be resisted ____________

e to sail completely round a region ____________

f watchful around all sides ____________

2 **Choose** suitable **words** from the word bank to **complete** these **sentences**.

a The region was ____________ for the villagers because of pollution.

b The creature became ____________ as it entered the thickly forested area.

c The children found that the toys on display were quite ____________.

d They tried to ____________ the laws but they were apprehended by the police.

e The ____________ of the submarine could not be seen easily.

3 **Add** suitable **endings** to the words in **bold** to **complete** these **sentences**.

a They entered the house after **unlock**________ the screen door.

b All the **impur**________ in the water made it unsafe to drink.

c The **circumnavig**________ of the island took six weeks.

☞ Answers on page 129

Prefixes

How much do you know?

1 **Join** the **prefixes** in the circle to the **word stems** in the box. **Write** the words.

trans ex
epi in dia
in mid mid
con per

pose	form	sist
lect	mit	vention
sult	stream	sode
	air	

______________________ ______________________

______________________ ______________________

______________________ ______________________

______________________ ______________________

______________________ ______________________

2 **Build** a word from the **prefix** shown in **bold** to complete each sentence.

- **a** The officers will **trans**______________ the money from the van to the safe.
- **b** The council will **im**____________ new water restrictions because of the drought.
- **c** The two groups made an **ar**_________________________ to share the money equally.
- **d** As he was **ex**____________________ the speed limit, he was caught by the traffic officer.

3 **Change** the words by **adding** one of these **endings**: *-ion*, *-ance*, *-er* or *-ic*.

- **a** translate ______________________ **b** perspire ______________________
- **c** perform ______________________ **d** emigrate ______________________
- **e** transmit ______________________ **f** construct ______________________

4 **Underline** the **prefix**. **Write** the **meaning**.

- **a** importer ______________________
- **b** repayment ______________________
- **c** transmit ______________________
- **d** comparison ______________________
- **e** epilogue ______________________
- **f** immaterial ______________________

5 **Draw** a **line** from the **word** to its **matching meaning**.

- **a** conflict — stick to
- **b** traverse — disagreement with another
- **c** adhere — travel across
- **d** midwinter — middle of the coldest months

☞ Answers on page 129

Review test 4

1 Are these statements about the **meanings of prefixes** true or false? Write **T** (true) or **F** (false).

- **a** In the word *intercede* the prefix means **between**. ______
- **b** The word *submarine* has a prefix which means **beneath**. ______
- **c** In the word *antagonist* **anti** means **against**. ______
- **d** *Precede* has a prefix that means **between**. ______
- **e** *Parasite* has a prefix that means **down**. ______
- **f** The word *attach* has a prefix that means **to**. ______

2 **Complete** the **words** from the meanings given.

- **a** to take into custody a______________t
- **b** copying writing across from one place to another t______________n
- **c** to shout or call out of e______________m
- **d** meeting of churchmen together s______________d
- **e** to rest back or again r______________e
- **f** not able to be read easily i______________e

3 **Form** new **nouns** from the following words using these **endings**: *-**ism***, *-**ion***, *-**or***, *-**er***, *-**ence*** and *-**ty***.

- **a** antagonist ______________ **b** supervisor ______________
- **c** prevent ______________ **d** extradite ______________
- **e** decelerate ______________ **f** oppress ______________
- **g** support ______________ **h** interfere ______________
- **i** abnormal ______________ **j** deflect ______________

4 **Add** or **change** a **prefix** to form words of **opposite meaning**.

- **a** downhill ______________ **b** happy ______________
- **c** probable ______________ **d** either ______________
- **e** import ______________ **f** valid ______________
- **g** tolerant ______________ **h** locked ______________

5 **Write** new words by **adding** or **changing** the **prefixes** in these words. Some prefixes you can use are ***re***-, ***un***-, ***dis***- and ***in***-.

- **a** content ______________ **b** improved ______________
- **c** inspect ______________ **d** protected ______________
- **e** equipped ______________ **f** member ______________
- **g** scientific ______________ **h** appealing ______________
- **i** service ______________ **j** version ______________
- **k** conscious ______________ **l** ability ______________
- **m** invited ______________ **n** direct ______________

Answers on page 129

Puzzle time 4

Crossword 4

Across

1 decrease in velocity
4 stop from happening
6 person who is against another
8 medicine to counteract poison
9 go down
12 article or item
13 look, control or check
15 go and settle in another country
20 turn away from
22 shut or keep in
23 something that travels under the sea
24 unable to put up with something

Down

2 words written on a tomb
3 not truthful or genuine
5 take between
7 keep for a later time
10 satisfied
11 distance around an object or area
14 discuss similarities and differences
16 between states
17 start of something
18 straight line drawn from one corner of a shape to the opposite corner
19 person who brings items into a country
21 sign

Wordsearch 4

There are ten words from Chapter 4 in this word search. They can be horizontal, vertical or diagonal. The words begin with the letters shown in the box on the left.

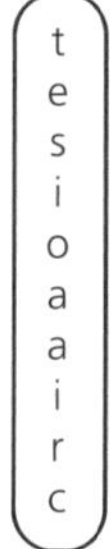

I	V	F	H	A	J	F	O	Z	W	P	T	E	K	U
N	Y	Y	U	T	J	Y	X	M	N	S	C	N	C	I
T	T	R	A	N	S	F	E	R	A	F	I	A	A	P
E	J	M	N	K	S	G	T	C	T	O	J	N	E	T
R	A	Q	L	F	P	D	T	I	J	A	G	T	S	X
W	D	E	N	N	H	U	H	E	V	C	T	O	C	V
E	G	S	L	R	O	L	R	A	W	O	V	N	O	V
A	J	X	A	N	W	O	I	Q	P	N	T	Y	Z	P
V	H	G	O	R	M	F	H	N	G	T	J	M	E	T
E	K	Y	N	Z	R	E	K	D	V	R	V	G	P	E
L	T	E	O	L	Y	I	V	K	M	A	P	E	P	J
G	P	S	L	M	D	C	V	B	E	B	D	H	G	E
X	R	K	F	G	L	R	A	E	Y	A	K	E	V	C
T	S	U	B	M	E	R	G	E	F	N	T	E	Z	T
W	I	J	W	L	Z	L	P	S	B	D	Q	M	W	K

Answers on pages 129–130

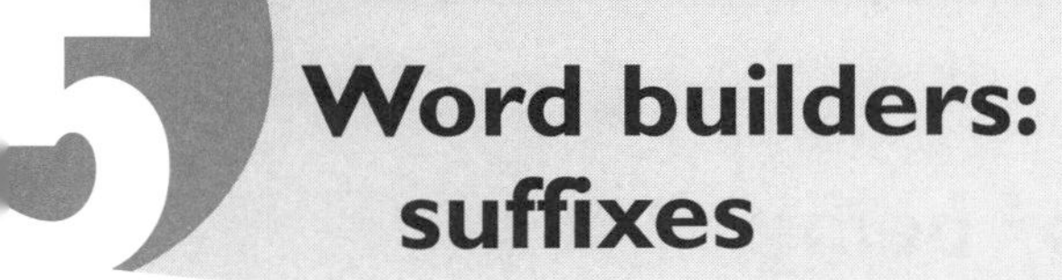

5 Word builders: suffixes

In this chapter, you will practise **building words** using **suffixes**.

- Suffixes are **word builders**.
- A suffix is a single letter or syllable that is added to the **end** of a word.
- Most of the suffixes in common use come from **Latin** and **Greek roots**.

Suffixes meaning *one who*

In this section, you will practise using **suffixes** that mean **one who**.

Suffix	Examples
-ar -er -or	begg**ar** = **one who** begs; bak**er** = **one who** bakes; sail**or** = **one who** sails
-ant	serv**ant** = **one who** serves
-ist	cycl**ist** = **one who** cycles
-eer -ier	engin**eer** = **one who** deals with engines glaz**ier** = **one who** deals with glass
-ee	employ**ee** = **one who** is employed
-an	electrici**an** = **one who** deals with electricity
-ic	crit**ic** = **one who** criticises

Word bank

-ar -er -or	schol**ar** li**ar** buy**er** build**er** lawy**er** act**or** govern**or** tail**or**
-ant -ist	assist**ant** merch**ant** botan**ist** art**ist** dent**ist** flor**ist**
-eer -ier -ee	mountain**eer** graz**ier** trust**ee**
-an -ian -ic	public**an** electric**ian** cler**ic** cyn**ic**

1 **Which words** from the word bank **match** these meanings?

a one who deals with the law ____________

b one who arranges and sells flowers ____________

c one who grazes animals for a living ____________

d one who owns or manages a hotel ____________

e one who is a member of the clergy ____________

2 **Choose** suitable **words** from the word bank to **complete** these **sentences**.

a The ____________ performed very well in the new film.

b All the clothes were made by the experienced ____________.

c The ____________ had been studying rare tropical plants for many years.

d The ____________ had to make sure that the money was used correctly.

e The old appliances were serviced regularly by the ____________.

3 **Change** the **nouns** in **bold** into **verbs** to complete these sentences.

a The three islands were (**governor**) ____________ by a chief on the main island.

b He (**assistant**) ____________ his brother to complete his homework.

c The young girl (**buyer**) ____________ the presents at a large department store yesterday.

d The film was very well (**actor**) ____________ by the experienced cast.

Answers on page 130

Suffixes meaning *state of being*

In this section, you will practise using **suffixes** that mean **state of being**.

Suffix		Examples
-y	**-ty**	miser**y** = **state of being** miserable; safe**ty** = **state of being** safe
-ice		not**ice** = **state of being** seen
-tude		grati**tude** = **state of being** grateful
-ure		capt**ure** = **state of being** caught
-age		cour**age** = **state of being** brave
-ance	**-ence**	ignor**ance** = **state of being** ignorant abs**ence** = **state of being** away
-th	**-t**	bread**th** = **state of being** broad gif**t** = **state of being** given
-hood		child**hood** = **state of being** a child
-ment		enjoy**ment** = **state of being** enjoyed
-ness		happi**ness** = **state of being** happy

Word bank

-y	**-ty**	luxur**y** victor**y** energ**y** hones**ty** cruel**ty** humili**ty**
-ice	**-tude**	coward**ice** just**ice** multi**tude** forti**tude**
-ure	**-age**	manufact**ure** advent**ure** marri**age** bond**age**
-ance	**-ence**	abund**ance** endur**ance** obedi**ence** pati**ence**
-th	**-t**	dep**th** heal**th** tru**th** heigh**t** thef**t**
-hood	**-ment**	woman**hood** brother**hood** content**ment** nourish**ment** kind**ness**
-ness		weak**ness** bright**ness**

1 **Which words** from the word bank above **match** these meanings?

a state of being sustained with food ____________

b state of being a great number of people ____________

c state of being humble ____________

d state of being well satisfied with life ____________

e state of being on a winning team ____________

2 **Choose** suitable **words** from the word bank to **complete** these **sentences**.

a The ____________ was held at the local church last Saturday.

b Many of the athletes were unable to complete the long ____________ race last week.

c When he returned the lost wallet, the boy was praised because of his ____________.

d The ____________ of the jewels took place late in the evening.

e The extreme ____________ of the sun was a problem for the desert people.

3 **Change** the words or part words into **adjectives** by using these suffixes: ***-ant***, ***-ous***, ***-ly***, ***-less*** or ***-t***.

a adventur ____________ b coward ____________

c obedien ____________ d victori ____________

e abund ____________ f weight ____________

☞ Answers on page 130

Suffixes meaning *to make or made of*

In this section, you will practise using **suffixes** that mean **to make** or **made of**.

Suffix	Example
-ate	renov**ate** = **to make** new again
-en	bright**en** = **to make** bright
-fy	beauti**fy** = **to make** beautiful
-le -se	dazz**le** = **to make** bright clean**se** = **to make** clean
-ish	dimin**ish** = **to make** smaller
-ise	fertil**ise** = **to make** fertile
-en	wooll**en** = **made of** wool

Word bank

-ate	abbrevi**ate** captiv**ate** agit**ate**
-en	rip**en** deep**en** fatt**en** height**en**
-fy	magni**fy** puri**fy** simpli**fy** recti**fy** glori**fy**
-le -se	spark**le** rust**le** start**le** rin**se**
-ish	nour**ish** publ**ish** van**ish** fin**ish** pol**ish**
-ise	bapt**ise** critic**ise** econom**ise** sympath**ise**
-en	gold**en** braz**en** lead**en** silk**en** wood**en**

1 **Which words** from the word bank above **match** these meanings?

a to make easy or simple ____________________

b to make or share feeling with others ____________________

c made of brass ____________________

d to make clearer ____________________

e to make available to the public ____________________

2 **Choose** suitable **words** from the word bank to **complete** these **sentences**.

a The machinery was used to ____________________ the excavation for the building.

b The new toys will ____________________ all the children who watched the exhibition.

c Because of increased costs, the company was forced to ____________________ on special events.

d The ____________________ cage had been carved out of Norfolk pine.

e The shiny silver plate will ____________________ in the sun.

3 **Change** the verbs into **nouns** using the suffixes ***-ism***, ***-ion***, ***-ment***, ***-er***, ***-ness*** and ***-y***.

a abbreviate ____________________ **b** nourish ____________________

c baptise ____________________ **d** polish ____________________

e economise ____________________ **f** ripen ____________________

Answers on page 130

Suffixes meaning *small*, *rather*, *like or direction*

In this section, you will practise using **suffixes** that mean **small**, **rather**, **like** or **direction**.

Suffix		Examples
-en	-et	chick**en** = **small** hen lock**et** = **small** lock
-let		leaf**let** = **small** piece of paper
-ling		seed**ling** = **small** growing seed
-ish		child**ish** = **like** a child
-y	-ey	bush**y** = **like** a bush clay**ey** = **like** clay
-ward	-wards	down**wards** = in the **direction** of down

Word bank

-en	-et	kitt**en** maid**en** lock**et** flower**et**
-let	-ling	rivu**let** stream**let** duck**ling** gos**ling**
-ish		fool**ish** Engl**ish** churl**ish** green**ish**
-y	-ey	cloud**y** dirt**y** hill**y** smok**y** storm**y**
-ward	-wards	back**ward** east**ward** sea**ward** to**wards**

1 **Which words** from the word bank above **match** these meanings?

a a tiny or small flower ____________

b rather or like being rude or impolite ____________

c rather or like a storm ____________

d in the direction of the sea or ocean ____________

e a small lock ____________

f rather or like a stupid person ____________

2 **Choose** suitable **words** from the word bank to **complete** these **sentences**.

a The small ____________ enjoyed running up and down the curtains.

b The severe storm changed the ____________ into a wide creek.

c The child was asked to change his ____________ shirt before the visitors arrived.

d The picnickers watched the ____________ skies anxiously.

e The goose and the ____________ were swimming on the dam.

3 **Add** suitable **endings** to the words in **bold** to complete these sentences.

a The boy realised that he had behaved **foolish**________ at the party.

b Because of the person's **childish**________, he was ordered to leave the room.

☞ Answers on page 130

Suffixes

1 **Join** the **suffixes** in the circle to the **word stems**. **Write** the words.

ward en
ness er or
ant en
ian let

inhabit	north	blind
magic	ring	strength
oat	shear	collect

______________ ______________ ______________
______________ ______________ ______________
______________ ______________ ______________

2 **Build words** to complete the sentences by **adding** a **suffix** to the word in **bold**.

- **a** Because of the **coarse**__________ of the cloth, the shirt was very uncomfortable to wear.
- **b** The small **drop**__________ of moisture had seeped into the space behind the window.
- **c** The **violin**__________ played the melody very well.
- **d** The cook had to **thick**__________ the mixture before pouring it into the baking dish.
- **e** Because of the **import**__________ of the meeting, all members were advised to attend.
- **f** The **invent**__________ had worked for many years to perfect the engine.
- **g** Because he was very **self**__________, he did not share any of the treats.

3 **Add** suitable **suffixes** to these words or word stems.

- **a** fever__________
- **b** ghost__________
- **c** exerc__________
- **d** refug__________
- **e** weal__________
- **f** jealous__________
- **g** nestl__________
- **h** safe__________

4 **Underline** the **suffixes** and **write** their **meanings**.

- **a** squatter ______________________________
- **b** energy ______________________________
- **c** refreshment ______________________________
- **d** merchant ______________________________
- **e** priesthood ______________________________
- **f** emperor ______________________________
- **g** truth ______________________________
- **h** leaden ______________________________

5 **Draw** a **line** from the **words** to their **meanings**.

a justice	one who studies
b settlement	state of being well off
c luxury	one who looks on
d scholar	state of being fair
e spectator	state of being settled

Answers on page 130

Suffixes meaning *full of, without or the act of*

In this section, you will practise using **suffixes** that mean **full of**, **without** or **the act of**.

Suffix	Examples
-ous	danger**ous** = **full of** danger
-ful	hope**ful** = **full of** hope
-less	care**less** = **without** care hope**less** = **without** hope
-ion	attract**ion** = **the act of** being attracted to something

Word bank

-ous	nerv**ous** graci**ous** glori**ous** furi**ous** cauti**ous** curi**ous**
-ful	cheer**ful** faith**ful** grace**ful** piti**ful** truth**ful**
-less	cease**less** harm**less** help**less** sense**less** thought**less**
-ion	sensat**ion** occas**ion** affect**ion** caut**ion** collect**ion**

1 **Which words** from the word bank above **match** these meanings?

a full of anger or strength ______________________

b full of happiness ______________________

c without stopping or interrupting ______________________

d the act of showing love or friendship ______________________

e without thinking ______________________

f full of care or attention ______________________

2 **Choose** suitable **words** from the word bank to **complete** these **sentences**.

a The ______________________ boy opened the box.

b The ______________________ dog remained at his owner's side throughout the night.

c Because of his ______________________ approach the valuable vase was not broken.

d The ______________________ noblewoman presented the prize.

e The artist created a ______________________ when she revealed her sculpture.

f The small snake was ______________________.

3 **Change** the words in **bold** into **adverbs** to suit these sentences.

a The girl always attended her ballet class (**cheerful**) ______________________.

b The stone bounced (**harmless**) ______________________ off the steel shutters.

c They greeted their relative (**affection**) ______________________.

d All the families would (**occasion**) ______________________ visit the town.

e The honest children spoke (**truthful**) ______________________.

☞ Answers on page 130

Suffixes meaning *relating to, belonging to, capable of* or *place where*

In this section, you will practise using **suffixes** that mean **relating to**, **belonging to**, **capable of** or **place where**.

Suffix	Examples
-ive	act**ive** = **relating to** action or movement
-al	annu**al** = **belonging to** a year
-ar	sol**ar** = **belonging to** the sun
-ic	publ**ic** = **belonging to** the people
-able -ible	enjoy**able** = **capable of** being enjoyed ed**ible** = **capable of** being eaten
-ary -ery -ory	libr**ary** = **place where** books are kept bak**ery** = **place where** bread is baked arm**ory** = **place where** arms (weapons) are kept

Word bank

-ive	nat**ive** expens**ive** object**ive** capt**ive** talkat**ive**
-al	fin**al** flor**al** leg**al** roy**al** decim**al** dent**al** mort**al**
-ar	lun**ar** simil**ar** singul**ar** popul**ar** circul**ar**
-ic	romant**ic** rust**ic** civ**ic** metall**ic**
-able	cur**able** lov**able** miser**able** comfort**able** peace**able**
-ible	aud**ible** flex**ible** horr**ible** terr**ible** leg**ible** vis**ible**
-ary	sanctu**ary** gran**ary** diction**ary** avi**ary**
-ery	gall**ery** nurs**ery** rock**ery** tann**ery** monast**ery**
-ory	direct**ory** dormit**ory** observat**ory** fact**ory**

1 **Which words** from the word bank above **match** these meanings?

- **a** relating to being made prisoner ____________________
- **b** belonging to the country ____________________
- **c** capable of being made well again ____________________
- **d** a place where birds are kept ____________________
- **e** a place where various goods are made ____________________
- **f** a place where young things are raised ____________________

2 **Choose** suitable **words** from the word bank to **complete** these **sentences**.

- **a** She bought a very ____________________ gift from the jewellers.
- **b** The ____________________ family gathered for the wedding of the young princess.
- **c** There was a barely ____________________ sound coming from the cabinet on the floor.
- **d** His handwriting was so bad that it was only just ____________________.

3 **Using** a **suffix**, change the words or part words in **bold** to fit these sentences.

- **a** The young model was **expensive**______ dressed for the television event.
- **b** All the Roman soldiers were taken into **captiv**______ after the battle.
- **c** The soldier was **mortal**______ wounded in the civil war.

Answers on page 130

Suffixes

1 **Join** the **suffixes** in the circle to the **word stems** in the box. **Write** the words.

ery ar
ion ful
able al less
ory ous
ible

nunn	incred	mov
adventur	rect	process
power	regul	tire
centr		

______________________ ______________________
______________________ ______________________
______________________ ______________________
______________________ ______________________
______________________ ______________________
______________________ ______________________

2 **Build** words to complete the sentences by **adding** a **suffix** to the words or word stems in **bold**.

- **a** The **cheer**________ players really enjoyed performing on the stage.
- **b** Because of his **sense**________ action the whole task had to be redone.
- **c** The centre of government was in the **capit**________ city of the state.
- **d** A **simil**________ number of people attended the last two days of the festival.

3 **Add** suitable **suffixes** to these words or word stems.

- **a** drink____________
- **b** api____________
- **c** fin____________
- **d** piti____________
- **e** cemet____________
- **f** leg____________

4 **Underline** the **suffixes** and write their **meanings**.

- **a** sorrowful ______________________
- **b** useless ______________________
- **c** attraction ______________________
- **d** singular ______________________
- **e** cosmic ______________________
- **f** invisible ______________________

5 **Draw a line from** the **word** to its **meaning**.

- **a** granary — capable of causing horror
- **b** popular — without bother or harm
- **c** harmless — belonging to the people
- **d** horrible — the act of making a donation
- **e** contribution — a place where grain is stored

☞ Answers on pages 130–131

Review test 5

1 Are these statements about the **meanings of suffixes** true or false? **Write T** (true) or **F** (false).

a In the word *merchant* the suffix means **one who**. ___________

b The word *cleric* has a suffix which means **to make**. ___________

c The suffix -***ence*** means **state of being**. ___________

d In the word *sisterhood* the suffix means **state of being**. ___________

e The suffixes -***le*** and -***se*** mean **made of**. ___________

f The suffix in the word *selection* means **the act of**. ___________

2 **Complete words** to **match** these meanings.

a a place of safety or refuge s______________y

b belong to a single one s______________r

c belong to ten d______________l

d the act of feeling or sensing c______________n

e full of care c______________s

f one who studies plant life b______________t

3 Use **suffixes** to form **nouns** from these words or word stems.

a build___________ b stream___________

c collect___________ d diction___________

e coward___________ f weak___________

g content___________ h capt___________

i mountain___________ j lock___________

k rock___________ l electric___________

4 **Change** these words to words of **opposite meaning** by changing the **suffixes**.

cheerless harmful pitiless thoughtful helpful

____

____

5 **Build** a word from the **suffix** in **bold** to complete the sentence.

a The ______________**ist** had arranged an attractive bouquet for the dancer.

b The ______________**er** discussed all the details of the case with his client.

c After the heavy rains there was an ________________**ance** of green grass for the animals.

d The explorers set off ________________**wards** the high mountain ranges.

Answers on page 131

Puzzle time 5

Crossword 5

Across

1 not able to be believed
3 cost or outlay
6 find fault with
9 person who deals with engines and machinery
13 place where birds are kept
15 happening at particular times
16 young duck
17 towards the sea
18 place of beauty or interest visited by tourists
19 unhappiness or grief

Down

2 full of danger
4 young plant raised from seed
5 condition in which expensive items are used and enjoyed
7 place where hides are tanned
8 full of good spirits
9 person who deals with electricity
10 person who governs
11 feed
12 able to be enjoyed
14 become smaller

1 I
6 C
5 L
8 C
15 R
18 A

Wordsearch 5

There are ten words from Chapter 5 in this word search. They can be horizontal, vertical or diagonal. The words begin with the letters shown in the box on the left.

L F T M R Y X Z A A Q W I U O
B O U Q L C R M S D N X L F E
V N V Z N I H E B B O V I G H
G C L O U D Y B I U Q G U G H
Y V W P I G B U A G Y M Q O X
P I S E R V A N T P B N Q L E
N S T H E F T R H L T Q C D M
A I H I F B W I I I U I I E D
D B O A T G B N P E G N S N H
G L N J K N G G C C Y R A E I
Z E E S E M P L O Y E E P R D
J H S R O Y S E R T F J V V R
E D T O J P S T D V W V R N B
J B Y F B S X B U X L J G Z J
S W I M C K X M H C C K T J A

Answers on page 131

6 Word origins: Latin and Greek roots

In this chapter, you will practise using words with **Latin** and **Greek roots**.

- Latin and Greek words are the **building blocks** for many English words. For example, *capable*, *capacity*, *captive*, *captivate* all come from the Latin *capio* (*I take*).
- Sometimes the word is so changed that it does **not closely resemble** the Latin root from which it is derived, e.g. *receipt*, *reception*, *recipient* are also from *capio*.
- When we say that *capio* is the **Latin root** of *capable*, we are saying it is the Latin word from which such syllables such as ***cap***, ***capt***, ***cip*** or ***cept*** are derived.
- **Use your dictionary** where necessary to help you complete the exercises in this chapter.

Roots relating to being – 1

In this section, you will practise words with these **Latin roots**:

ago = I do or act ***audio*** = I hear ***cado*** = I fall ***curro*** = I run

Word banks

A	***ago***	action actor agent transaction inactive overact transact counteract active agile act
B	***audio***	audience audible inaudible audiometer audition auditorium
C	***cado***	accident cascade decay occasional casual deciduous cadence
D	***curro***	courier current corridor courser occur recur incur cursive cursory

1 **Choose words** from the word banks above to **match** these meanings.

a relating to not acting A ______
b a place to hear music B ______
c a stretch of falling water C ______
d a fast horse D ______
e letters running together D ______
f fall or break down C ______
g not able to be heard B ______
h one who acts for another person A ______

2 In the word banks **find words** that are **antonyms** of the following words.

a inactive ______ **b** audible ______ **c** formal ______
d past ______ **e** frequent ______ **f** evergreen ______

3 In the word banks **find words** that are **synonyms** of the following words.

a happen ______ **b** informal ______ **c** lively ______
d mishap ______ **e** decompose ______ **f** passageway ______

4 **a** Write a **noun**, **adjective** and **adverb** from the verb *act*. ______
b Write the **past tense** and **present tense** of the verb *occur*. ______
c Write an **adjective** and an **adverb** from the noun *accident*. ______

Answers on page 131

Roots relating to being – 2

In this section, you will practise words with these **Latin roots**:

tendo = I stretch ***credo*** = I believe ***video*** = I see ***teneo*** = I hold

Word banks

A	***tendo***	tension extension extend intend pretend distend extensive intense
B	***credo***	creed credit creditor discredit credible incredible incredulous
C	***video***	evidence surveyor view revise supervise evident visible visual
D	***teneo***	tenant tenacity continent contain entertain retain sustain tenacious

1 **Select words** from the word banks above to **match** these meanings.

a the act of stretching out A ________________________

b able to be believed B ________________________

c to see or learn again C ________________________

d to hold back or again D ________________________

e stretched out A ________________________

f something that is believed B ________________________

g able to be seen C ________________________

h one who holds a lease on property D ________________________

2 **Add endings** to the words or part words in **bold** to complete these sentences.

a The ship was **extensive**_______ damaged in the cyclone.

b This boy has not been **credit**_______ with helping to save the swimmers.

c The teacher said that the **revis**_______ of the work was quite important.

d All of the **supervis**_______ had checked the building for faults.

e The half-time **entertain**_______ at the football game was very colourful.

3 In the word banks **find words** that are **antonyms** of these words.

a shorten ____________________ **b** credit ____________________

c invisible ____________________ **d** discard ____________________

e unbelievable ____________________ **f** bore ____________________

4 In the word banks **find words** that are **synonyms** of these words.

a leaseholder ____________________ **b** include ____________________

c simulate ____________________ **d** hold ____________________

e determined ____________________ **f** support ____________________

5 **a** Write a **verb**, **adjective** and **adverb** built from the noun *extension*.

____

b Write a **noun** and an **adjective** from the verb *supervise*.

____

c Write **two nouns** built from the verb *entertain*.

____

☞ Answers on page 131

Roots relating to being – 3

In this section, you will practise words with these **Latin roots**:
dico = I say ***verto*** = I turn ***spiro*** = I breathe ***capio*** = I take

Word banks

A	***dico***	dictator dictionary verdict dictate contradict predict indicate indicative
B	***verto***	conversion inversion conversation advertisement invert convert advertise reversible
C	***spiro***	perspiration respiration conspirator perspire expire conspire
D	***capio***	captive captor participant receipt accept capture intercept capable

1 **Select words** from the word banks above to **match** these meanings.

- **a** to say something against A ______
- **b** something that turns people towards something B ______
- **c** the act of breathing in and out C ______
- **d** one who takes a prisoner D ______
- **e** to take between D ______
- **f** to breathe through the skin C ______
- **g** able to be turned back B ______
- **h** to say before an event happens A ______

2 **Add endings** to the words or part words in **bold** to complete these sentences.

- **a** This type of work is not regarded as **accept**______.
- **b** All the **conspir**______ met in the cave to plan their attack.
- **c** The **advertise**______ hoped that they would sell many thousands of their products.
- **d** The **indicat**______ on the machine did not show there was a problem.
- **e** She bought a brand new **convert**______ after trading in her old car.

3 In the word banks **find words** that are **synonyms** of these words.

- **a** autocrat ______ **b** argue ______
- **c** foretell ______ **d** dialogue ______
- **e** show ______ **f** transform ______

4 In the word banks **find words** that are **antonyms** of these words.

- **a** reject ______ **b** release ______
- **c** incompetent ______ **d** survive ______
- **e** agree ______ **f** conceal ______

5 **a** Write an **adjective** and **noun** from the verb *convert*.

______

b Write a **noun** and an **adjective** from the verb *accept*.

______

c Write a **noun** and an **adjective** from the verb *contradict*.

______

☞ Answers on page 132

Roots relating to being – 4

In this section, you will practise words with these **Latin roots**:
scribo = I write ***sto*** = I stand ***specto*** = I see ***tango*** = I touch

Word banks

A	***scribo***	manuscript prescription postscript description scribble transcribe subscribe descriptive
B	***sto***	obstacle statement station statue contrast obstinate stable stationary
C	***specto***	inspector prospector spectacle inspect prospect suspect conspicuous spectacular
D	***tango***	tact tangent attain contact contagious tangible

1 **Select words** from the word banks above to match these meanings.

- **a** something written by hand A __________
- **b** something that stands in the way B __________
- **c** easily seen C __________
- **d** a line that touches a curve D __________
- **e** to touch or reach something through effort D __________
- **f** someone seen as possibly involved in a crime C __________
- **g** something that stands firmly B __________
- **h** something written after a letter is completed A __________

2 **Add endings** to the words or part words in **bold** to complete these sentences.

- **a** The student wrote a **descript**________ account of the area.
- **b** The boy offended many people because he was so **tact**________.
- **c** They **suspect**________ that the youth had been involved in the robbery.
- **d** The **contrast**________ colours in the painting made it particularly attractive.
- **e** The girl took out a **subscri**________ to the popular magazine.

3 In the word banks **find words** that are **antonyms** of these words.

- **a** liken __________ **b** fail __________
- **c** non-infectious __________ **d** untouchable __________
- **e** unimpressive __________ **f** shaky __________

4 In the word banks **find words** that are **synonyms** of these words.

- **a** evident __________ **b** discretion __________
- **c** wilful __________ **d** still __________
- **e** magnificent __________ **f** scene __________

5
- **a** Write a **verb**, **adjective** and **adverb** from the noun *suspect*. __________
- **b** Write a **noun** and an **adjective** from the verb *attain*. __________
- **c** Write **adverbs** from these two adjectives: *conspicuous*, *spectacular*.

____

☞ Answers on page 132

Words and word origins

How much do you know?

1 Answer **T** (true) or **F** (false) for the following statements.

a ***Overact*** means to act above the normal method. ________

b An **audiometer** is used to measure hearing. ________

c The word ***occasionally*** means infrequently. ________

d A **creditor** is one who is owed money. ________

e A synonym for ***tenacity*** is ***determination***. ________

f One who takes part is called a **captive**. ________

g To turn upside down is to **convert** something. ________

h The words ***conspicuous*** and ***spectacular*** are antonyms. ________

2 **Number** these words 1–10 in **alphabetical order**.

audience ____ active ____ accident ____ actor ____
agent ____ attain ____ agile ____ advertise ____
accept ____ action ____

3 Which of these words are **misspelt**? **Mark** them with a cross (**x**) and **rewrite** them correctly on the lines below.

transacton ___ inaudable ___ auditorum ___ occur ___
entertain ___ continint ___ credable ___ advertisement ___
acept ___ capter ___ intrecept ___ supervise ___

____

____

____

4 **Complete** the table.

	Noun	Verb	Adjective
a		extend	
b			supervisory
c		dictate	
d	conversion		
e			descriptive

5 **Add prefixes** and **suffixes** to the words in the box to build new words to **complete** the **sentences**.

spectacle reverse capture occasion agent
prescribe respire distend current revise

a The winter coat was ______________________ and could be used in dry or wet weather.

b The children had contracted a ______________________ tract infection.

c After ______________________ the enemy soldiers, the troops marched them away.

d The officials were ______________________ unavailable because they were on leave.

Answers on page 132

Roots relating to actions and movements – 1

In this section, you will practise words with these **Latin roots**:
facio = I make ***jacio*** = I throw ***flecto*** = I bend ***pendeo*** = I hang

Word banks

A	***facio***	factory factor satisfaction benefactor manufacture disinfect sacrifice beneficial
B	***jacio***	adjective interjection object projectile inject project dejected objectionable
C	***flecto***	reflection reflector inflection deflect flexible reflective
D	***pendeo***	pendant pendulum pennant depend suspend independent

1 **Select words** from the word banks above to **match** these meanings.

- **a** place where things are made A ______________
- **b** something thrown forward B ______________
- **c** to bend or turn aside C ______________
- **d** the part of a clock that hangs down D ______________
- **e** something that hangs around the neck D ______________
- **f** the act of bending back again C ______________
- **g** to throw into B ______________
- **h** one who does good for others A ______________

2 **Add endings** to the words in **bold** to complete these sentences.

- **a** Because the work was not done **satisfact**__________ it had to be redone.
- **b** The liquid **disinfect**__________ was used to ensure that the area was germ-free.
- **c** The **flexib**__________ of the material made it very useful for filling gaps in the brick work.
- **d** The worker was praised by the supervisor for her **depend**__________.
- **e** The **inject**__________ was needed to prevent the infection spreading rapidly.
- **f** This fine example of a **suspens**__________ bridge was built earlier this century.

3 In the word banks **find words** that are **antonyms** of these words.

- **a** dissatisfaction ______________ **b** happy ______________
- **c** pleasing ______________ **d** rigid ______________

4 **Add** the **prefixes** and **suffixes** given to the word in **bold**.

- **a** dis s ed ing ant **infect**: ______________

____

____

- **b** dis es ed ing ion ory arily **satisfy**: __________

____

____

5 **Write** the **past tense** and an **adjective** from the verb *sacrifice*.

____

☞ Answers on page 132

Roots relating to actions and movements – 2

In this section, you will practise words with these **Latin roots**:
moveo = I move ***rego*** = I rule ***pono*** = I place ***claudo*** = I shut

Word banks

A	***moveo***	locomotive motor commotion promotion promote remove mobile movable
B	***rego***	regiment director regent region direct regulate incorrect irregular
C	***pono***	opponent depot impostor preposition compose dispose deposit oppose opposite positive
D	***claudo***	conclusion clause recluse conclude include disclose exclusive inclusive

1 **Select words** from the word banks above to **match** these meanings.

- **a** the act of moving forward A ______
- **b** one who rules a kingdom for another person B ______
- **c** one who is placed against another C ______
- **d** the art of ending something D ______
- **e** one who shuts himself or herself away D ______
- **f** to place together C ______
- **g** one who rules or controls B ______
- **h** able to be moved A ______

2 **Add endings** to the words or part words in **bold** to complete these sentences.

- **a** All the people were involved in the **promotion**______ activities at the centre.
- **b** All the **regulat**______ about water usage had been sent out.
- **c** The musical **compos**______ had been working on the sonata for several months.
- **d** Because the evidence was not **conclu**______ the suspects were set free.
- **e** Because of a serious infection the young girl had reduced **mobil**______ for several months.
- **f** The **dispos**______ of the rubbish from the building site took several days.

3 In the word banks **find words** that are **antonyms** of these words.

- **a** regular ______ **b** negative ______
- **c** exclude ______ **d** demote ______
- **e** indirect ______ **f** silence ______

4 In the word banks **find words** that are **synonyms** of these words.

- **a** disorder ______ **b** discard ______
- **c** instruct ______ **d** resist ______
- **e** devise ______ **f** definite ______

5 **a** Write a **noun** and **adjective** from the verb *oppose*. ______

b Write a **noun**, **adjective** and **adverb** from the verb *conclude*.

______

c Write a **verb** and **adverb** from the adjective *exclusive*. ______

☞ Answers on page 132

Roots relating to actions and movements – 3

In this section, you will practise words with these **Latin roots**:
cedo = I go ***pello*** = I drive ***duco*** = I lead or draw along ***struo*** = I build

Word banks

A	***cedo***	ancestor procession antecedent proceed exceed successful accessible
B	***pello***	propeller propulsion impel compel impulsive compulsory expel
C	***duco***	conductor education production reduction educate introduce productive
D	***struo***	construction structure destroyer instruct obstruct constructive destructive

1 **Select words** from word banks above to **match** these meanings.

- **a** one who goes before you A ______
- **b** to drive out B ______
- **c** the act of leading to knowledge C ______
- **d** relating to building D ______
- **e** something that is built D ______
- **f** one who leads a group together C ______
- **g** the act of driving forward B ______
- **h** to go beyond the normal A ______

2 **Add endings** to the words in **bold** to complete these sentences.

- **a** All the work he had done was completed **successful**______.
- **b** The **education**______ textbooks were used by the students.
- **c** The **instruct**______ that the boy received enabled him to complete the project.
- **d** Because the child acted **impulsive**______ he was sorry for his actions.
- **e** The court of law followed a particular **proce**______ when it was in session.
- **f** The police officer stated that the accident was due to **exces**______ speed.

3 In the word banks **find words** that are **antonyms** of these words.

- **a** rehearsed ______ **b** invite ______
- **c** unapproachable ______ **d** retreat ______

4 **Add** the **prefixes** and **suffixes** given to the words in **bold**. Write the new words.

- **a** un ful fully ion **success**: ______
- **b** in ion ible ibly **access**: ______

5 Write a **noun** made from each of these words.

process ______ instruct ______

☞ Answers on page 132

Roots relating to actions and movements – 4

In this section, you will practise words with these **Latin roots**:
traho = I draw ***mitto*** = I send ***colo*** = I till ***fundo*** = I pour

Word banks

A	***traho***	tractor portrait contractor attraction extract subtract attractive
B	***mitto***	message missile missionary transmitter dismiss emit remit transmit
C	***colo***	colony agriculture culture cultivation colonise cultivate cultural colonial
D	***fundo***	transfusion confusion fusion foundry confuse refuse profusion refusal

1 **Select words** from the word banks to **match** these meanings.

- **a** something that draws other machinery A ______________
- **b** words that are sent B ______________
- **c** the act of tilling the soil C ______________
- **d** the act of pouring across D ______________
- **e** the act of pouring forwards (in quantity) D ______________
- **f** to till the soil C ______________
- **g** to send across B ______________
- **h** to draw out of A ______________

2 **Add endings** to the words in **bold** to complete these sentences.

- **a** The painting she bought was so **attract**______________ that she couldn't wait to exhibit it in her home.
- **b** The control of **emi**______________ from the factory was difficult to accomplish.
- **c** The **transmi**______________ of the serious illness was monitored by the scientists.
- **d** The student found that the **agricultur**______________ subjects were very interesting.
- **e** The different instructions caused a lot of **confus**______________.
- **f** The **extract**______________ of the metals from the ore was a lengthy process.

3 **Write nouns** made from these words.

- **a** portrait ______________
- **b** subtract ______________
- **c** contract ______________
- **d** attract ______________

4 In the word banks **find words** that are **synonyms** of these words.

- **a** release ______________
- **b** appealing ______________
- **c** discharge ______________
- **d** reimburse ______________
- **e** settlement ______________
- **f** smelting ______________

5 **a** Write an **adjective** and **verb** from the word *colony*.

____

b Write an **adjective**, **noun** and **adverb** from *attract*.

____

☞ Answers on pages 132–133

Roots relating to actions and movements – 5

In this section, you will practise words with these **Latin roots**:
lego = I gather, read or select ***peto*** = I seek ***fluo*** = I flow ***pleo*** = I fill

Word banks

A	***lego***	election lecturer selection legend collect elect neglect legible select
B	***peto***	petition competition repetition compete repeat impetuous competent repeat
C	***fluo***	confluence fluid influence fluent superfluous fluorescent
D	***pleo***	complement implement supplement complete deplete accomplish

1 **Select words** from the word banks above to **match** these meanings.

- **a** the act of choosing A ____________
- **b** to seek or do again B ____________
- **c** flowing light C ____________
- **d** to fill or end something D ____________
- **e** something that completes or fills D ____________
- **f** state of flowing together C ____________
- **g** the act of seeking or doing again B ____________
- **h** able to be read A ____________

2 **Add endings** to the words in **bold** to complete these sentences.

- **a** The worker was praised for his **legend**____________ work in improving the health of the disadvantaged communities.
- **b** All the **compet**____________ in the event had trained very hard for several months.
- **c** Because of his **incompet**____________ he failed to finish the job satisfactorily.
- **d** His **fluen**____________ in several languages was a wonderful advantage in his work.
- **e** The **influen**____________ community leader called the meeting to discuss the health crisis.
- **f** The **deplet**____________ of oil reserves in the country was a serious problem.

3 **Change** these words to make **adverbs**.

- **a** competent ____________ **b** impetuous ____________
- **c** compete ____________ **d** legible ____________

4 In the word banks **find words** that are **synonyms** of these words.

- **a** gather ____________ **b** impulsive ____________
- **c** exhaust ____________ **d** capable ____________
- **e** ignore ____________ **f** choose ____________

5 **a** Write a **verb**, **adjective** and **adverb** from *collection*.

____

b Write a **noun**, **adjective** and **adverb** from *repeat*.

____

Answers on page 132

Words and word origins

How much do you know?

1 Answer **T** (true) or **F** (false) for the following statements.

- **a** A comment thrown into a discussion or speech is an **interjection**. ______
- **b** To bend something down or away is to **deflect** it. ______
- **c** Something that flows is said to be **superfluous**. ______
- **d** A synonym for ***flexible*** is ***pliable***. ______
- **e** An **impostor** is one who takes the place of another. ______
- **f** Another name for a **recluse** is a hermit. ______
- **g** The opposite of ***construct*** is ***instruct***. ______
- **h** The meeting place of two flowing rivers is the **confluence**. ______

2 **Which** of the three words would come **first** in a dictionary?

- **a** repetition, repeat, regularly ____________________
- **b** conductor, construction, consider ____________________
- **c** propeller, propulsion, promotion ____________________
- **d** inflection, injection, innocent ____________________

3 **Mark** the words that are **misspelt** with a cross (**x**) and **write** them correctly on the lines below.

benefacter ___	flexable ___	suspension ___
exclusive ___	regulated ___	producton ___
coloniel ___	competant ___	legible ___

____

____

____

4 **Complete** the table.

	Noun	Verb	Adjective
a		satisfy	
b			reflective
c		conclude	
d	education		
e		repeat	

5 **Add prefixes** and **suffixes** to the words in the box to **complete** the sentences.

object	proceed	tractor	cultivation
regulate	propel	transmit	profuse

- **a** It was a ____________________ that no animals were allowed on the freeway.
- **b** The ____________________ wound its way from the centre of the town to the showgrounds.
- **c** The craft was ____________________ across the lake by a powerful engine.
- **d** There was a ____________________ of wild flowers on display on the plains.

Answers on page 133

Roots relating to the body – 1

In this section, you will practise words with these **Latin roots**:
anima = life or breath ***cor*** = heart ***corpus*** = body ***manus*** = hand

Word banks

A	***anima***	animal animation animate inanimate
B	***cor***	core courage discourage encourage cordial courageous discouragement
C	***corpus***	corpse corps corporation incorporate corpulent
D	***manus***	manacle manager manuscript manage manufacture manual

1 **Select words** from the word banks above to **match** these meanings.

a having life or breath A ______________
b to make or put heart into someone B ______________
c a group or body of soldiers C ______________
d a document written by hand D ______________
e to make by hand D ______________
f to include or be included in a united body C ______________
g full of heart or bravery B ______________
h not having life or breath A ______________

2 **Add endings** to the words in **bold** to complete these sentences.

a The children were given a great deal of **encourage**__________ to complete the work well.
b Although outnumbered, the soldiers fought **courage**__________ against the large force.
c They were all **cordial**__________ invited to the party held over the weekend.
d The **manage**__________ of the company had decided to provide the workers with a new recreation area.
e The electric gate on the block could also be opened **manual**__________.
f The young woman reached a **manage**__________ position within a few years of joining the firm.

3 In the word banks **find words** that are **antonyms** of these words.

a cowardice ______________ **b** mismanage ______________
c living ______________ **d** discourteous ______________
e automatic ______________ **f** encouragement ______________

4 **Add *ed*** and ***ing*** to these verbs.

a manage ______________ ______________
b encourage ______________ ______________
c incorporate ______________ ______________

5 Write a **verb**, **adjective** and **adverb** built from the noun *courage*.

____

____

☞ Answers on page 133

Roots relating to the body – 2

In this section, you will practise words with these **Latin** and **Greek roots**:
dens = tooth ***pes*** = foot ***caput*** = head ***bios*** = life

Word banks

A	***dens***	dentist dentistry trident indent dental indented
B	***pes***	biped quadruped pedal pedestrian impede
C	***caput***	capital captain precipice decapitate chief
D	***bios***	biography autobiography biology microbe amphibious

1 **Select words** from the word banks above to **match** these meanings.

a the study of dental treatment A ____________________
b a creature moving on two feet B ____________________
c to remove the head C ____________________
d the study of life D ____________________
e a self-written life story D ____________________
f one who is the head or chief C ____________________
g to place a foot in the way of something B ____________________
h an implement with three teeth A ____________________

2 **Add endings** to the words in **bold** to complete these sentences.

a The children **pedal**______________ quickly across the park to the station.
b The fallen power pole was **imped**______________ the progress of the traffic.
c The short **biograph**______________ sketch of the famous artist was quite interesting.
d The **decapitat**______________ of the prisoners was a serious war crime.
e All the children received **dent**______________ treatment at the local clinic.
f The **indent**______________ was drawn up and signed by the apprentice and the employer.

3 **Write two meanings** for the word *indent*. Use your dictionary.

____

____

4 What is the **difference** between a **biography** and an **autobiography**?

____

____

5 **Write** a **verb** and **noun** from the word *capital*.

____

____

☞ Answers on page 133

Roots relating to objects, places and numbers – 1

In this section, you will practise words with these **Latin roots**:
finis = end ***terra*** = earth ***unus*** = one ***decem*** = ten

Word banks

A	***finis***	final finale finish define refine confine superfine unfinished
B	***terra***	terrace territory inter Mediterranean subterranean
C	***unus***	union unit universe uniform unite unity universal unanimous
D	***decem***	decade December decimal decimate

1 **Select words** from the word banks above to **match** these meanings.

a the end to a piece of music A ______________________
b underneath the earth B ______________________
c to make as one C ______________________
d a period of ten years D ______________________
e relating to ten D ______________________
f of one mind C ______________________
g to place into the earth B ______________________
h to end someone's freedom A ______________________

2 **Add endings** to the words and part words in **bold** to complete these sentences.

a The teacher asked the class for a **defin**____________ of the word *unanimous*.
b The pop group was **univers**____________ admired by young people.
c During the long battle the losing side was **decimat**____________.
d The sugar cane was turned into pure white sugar at the **refine**____________ on the outskirts of town.
e The governments should create **uniform**____________ in the size and colour of traffic signals.
f The **unif**____________ of all the states in the country came about last year.

3 **Change** these words to **nouns**.

confine ____________ unite ____________ final ____________

4 In the word banks **find words** that are **antonyms** of these words.

a begin ____________________ **b** separate ____________________
c completed ____________________

5 **Complete** the table, giving two parts of the verb and the noun built from it.

Today	Yesterday	I am ________	Noun
a I confine			
b I unite			

☞ Answers on page 133

Roots relating to objects, places and numbers – 2

In this section, you will practise words with these **Latin roots**:
civis = citizen ***aequus*** = equal ***populus*** = people ***centum*** = hundred

Word banks

A	***civis***	civilian citizen city civics civilise civil
B	***aequus***	equality equator equinox equation equal equalise equate equilateral equable
C	***populus***	population populace populate depopulate populous public publish republic
D	***centum***	cent century centipede centenary centurion

1 **Select words** from the word banks above to **match** these meanings.

- **a** the study of citizenship A ______
- **b** a line that divides the earth into two equal parts B ______
- **c** to bring the population down C ______
- **d** a period of a hundred years D ______
- **e** an officer in charge of 100 Roman soldiers D ______
- **f** relating to civil life A ______
- **g** a triangle with three equal sides B ______
- **h** relating to being a citizen A ______

2 **Add endings** to the words in **bold** to complete these sentences.

- **a** The Roman **civil**_______ extended throughout the Mediterranean and southern Europe.
- **b** The mathematical **equat**_______ that the students completed was quite complex.
- **c** All the **populat**_______ areas suffered greatly in the cyclone.
- **d** It took many **centur**_______ for the forests to grow back entirely.
- **e** The rude stranger did not speak **civil**_______ to the townspeople when he arrived.
- **f** The island in the Pacific was well known for its **equa**_______ climate.

3 **Form nouns** from these words.

civil ______
civilise ______
equalise ______
populate ______

4 **Write** the **past tense** of these verbs.

equalise ______
civilise ______
populate ______
publish ______

5 In the word box **find words** that are **antonyms** of these words.

- **a** unequal ______ **b** discourteous ______

Answers on page 133

Roots relating to objects, places and numbers – 3

In this section, you will practise words with these **Greek roots**:
polis = city ***phos*** = light ***logos*** = discourse or study ***micros*** = small

Word banks

A	***polis***	policy politics political metropolis metropolitan
B	***phos***	phosphorus photograph photocopier photosynthesis photogenic
C	***logos***	geology ornithology prologue dialogue epilogue eulogy zoology chronological
D	***micros***	microbe micrometer microscope microwave microphone microfilm

1 **Select words** from the word banks above to **match** these meanings.

- **a** relating to a large city A ________________
- **b** machine that copies documents B ________________
- **c** study of the rocks of the earth C ________________
- **d** very small living creature D ________________
- **e** instrument for making small sounds louder D ________________
- **f** study of animals C ________________
- **g** picture taken with light B ________________
- **h** study of cities and states A ________________

2 **Add endings** to the words and part words in **bold** to complete these sentences.

- **a** **Political**____________, it was a very difficult problem for the government to solve.
- **b** The naturalist had studied **photograph**____________ at a college for visual arts.
- **c** The unusual rock and ash was a surprising **geolog**____________ find.
- **d** The **microscop**____________ organisms were discovered at a great depth in the ocean.
- **e** The young girl, who had loved birds all her life, became a famous **ornitholog**____________.
- **f** The **zoolog**____________ in charge of the section worked through the night to save the injured animal.

3 What is an **anthology**?

____

4 What is a **photometer**?

____

5 What is a **microsecond**?

____

6 What is **microbiology**?

____

☞ Answers on pages 133–134

Roots relating to objects, places and numbers – 4

In this section, you will practise words with these **Greek roots**:
phone = sound ***ge*** = earth ***metron*** = measure ***chronos*** = time

Word banks

A	***phone***	gramophone phonics telephone phonetic telephonic phoneme phonology
B	***ge***	geography geology geometry geometric
C	***metron***	barometer chronometer micrometer perimeter thermometer
D	***chronos***	chronicle chronometer synchronise chronic chronology chronological

1 **Select words** from the word banks above to **match** these meanings.

- **a** study of speech sounds A ______________________
- **b** study of the regions of the earth B ______________________
- **c** tool to measure very small objects C ______________________
- **d** to keep time together D ______________________
- **e** in the correct order in time D ______________________
- **f** measurement around a shape C ______________________
- **g** study of shapes and measurement B ______________________
- **h** simple sound in a language A ______________________

2 **Add endings** to the words in **bold** to complete these sentences.

- **a** The professor had carried out a **phonolog**______________ study of the sound systems of the newly discovered language.
- **b** The **geolog**______________ made an impressive study of the Pacific rim of fire.
- **c** The **baromet**______________ pressure had been falling rapidly, indicating a weather change.
- **d** The **synchronis**______________ of all the clocks was completed before the test session.
- **e** The boy was **chronic**______________ ill with asthma.
- **f** The child had difficulty spelling the unusual words **phonetic**______________.

3 What is a **gramophone** or **phonograph**?

____

4 What is a **photomontage**?

____

5 What is a **chronicle**?

____

6 **Form adjectives** from these words.

meteorology ______________________ geometry ______________________

Answers on page 134

Words and word origins

How much do you know?

1 Answer **T** (true) or **F** (false) for the following statements.

a One who supervises the work at hand is a **manager**. ______

b Something that does not have life is **animate**. ______

c A **corps** is a group of soldiers. ______

d Objects to limit hand movement are called **manuals**. ______

e The head person is called a **chief**. ______

f **Biology** is the study of life. ______

2 Mark the **misspelt words** with a cross (**x**) and **write** them correctly on the lines below.

geolegy ____ politicel ____ photogenic ____

microscopic ____ geometrical ____ corportaton ____

encourige ____ pedistrian ____ universaly ____

____

____

3 **Complete** the table.

Noun	Verb	Adjective	Adverb
a courage			
b		civil	
c	equalise		
d		public	
e definition			

4 **Circle** the words that are **not related** to the Latin or Greek root given in **bold**.

a ***finis*** (end) finite refining fiord confinement

b ***populus*** (people) popular porcelain depopulate porous

c ***phos*** (light) photostat photoelectric phonetic phobia

d ***micros*** (small) microsecond microprint mica microchip

e ***chronos*** (time) chromatic chronology chronic chromium

f ***ge*** (the earth) geocentric geographical georgette geographical

5 Use the words in the box to **build words** to **complete** the **sentences**.

encourage unify civil century equal microscope

a All the students were given ______________________ to finish the work on time.

b The courteous operator was well known for his ______________________ to all the other workers.

c The boys were all held ______________________ responsible for the damage to the fence.

d The ______________________ organisms could only be viewed with a powerful piece of equipment.

Answers on page 134

Review test 6

1 Are the statements about the meanings of these Latin and Greek roots **true** or **false**? Answer **T** (true) or **F** (false).

a The word *audition* is built from *audio*, meaning *I hear*. ______

b *Corridor* is built from *curro*, meaning *I run*. ______

c The word *tenant* is derived from *tendo*, meaning *I stretch*. ______

d The word *invert* is derived from *verto*, meaning *I turn*. ______

e *Capture* is built from the Latin root *capio*, meaning *I take*. ______

2 **Complete** the **words** to suit the meanings given. Use a dictionary.

a not able to be believed in____________________e

b full of the capacity to hold on te____________________s

c to breathe through the skin pe____________________e

d something that is written after po____________________t

3 **Form nouns** from these words.

a object ____________________ b deflect ____________________

c suspend ____________________ d oppose ____________________

4 **Build** a **word** from the Latin root in **bold** to complete the sentence.

a It was clearly (***video***) ____________________ that the children had been swimming in the pool.

b The neighbours often had a (***verto***) ____________________ when they met at the shopping centre.

c The clever piece of (***scribo***) ____________________ writing made it easy for us to visualise the scene.

d The (***flecto***) ____________________ wire was used to wrap up the equipment securely.

e The traffic accident was a major (***struo***) ____________________ and it was several hours before the road was clear.

5 Mark the **misspelt words** with a cross (**x**) and **write** them correctly on the lines below.

continint ___ credable ___ reversible ___

pennant ___ incapable ___ imposter ___

missionary ___ impetuous ___ pedestrin ___

____

____

6 Use the words in the box to **build new words** to **complete** the sentences.

unify	audible	revise	regulate	dispose	attractive

a The noise in the pipe was so faint it was almost ____________________.

b All the students were asked to ensure that their ____________________ of the work was thorough.

c They had no idea how to draw up the ____________________ for the new club.

Answers on page 134

Puzzle time 6

Crossword 6

Across

3 act of tilling the soil
4 act of moving forward
5 do more than is required
7 small waterfall
9 throw forward
13 something seen or heard in a trial
16 large and far-reaching
17 very large land mass
18 person who rules alone
19 act of being heard when trying out for a task or part
20 sculptured figure

Down

1 make or build by hand
2 something that drives a ship forward
6 person who is captured
8 instructions written by a doctor
10 able to be bent
11 person opposed to someone
12 make known
14 act against something
15 something thrown or fired into the air

Wordsearch 6

There are ten words from Chapter 6 in this word search. They can be horizontal, vertical or diagonal. The words begin with the letters shown in the box on the left.

e s o r c r f c c f

Z P M C D F G R C U R S O R Y
E M U W G B I H E C W J Q D I
B R E F U S A L W C F D Q G X
B P S V A W F T W A L E Y N T
O B W X R V E V F D N U D T L
C C W B Z N H Q K H X F S W Y
C O A S U C C E S S F U L E T
A N V W C A P A B L E M A P M
S T U T V F A C T O R Q U I L
I A R K X P K U H Z R C M W B
O C E Z M C P O W Y B C S E Q
N T V X T V N Z F O T E D W W
A K T B P I X Z P K C O X Y Q
L M F J D E N E B Y K U M W V
W Z B V E T L H F L U I D A W

Answers on page 134

Reference section

A Spelling list

Aborigine
accept
accessible
accident
accommodate
accompany
achievement
activity
advertise
advertisement
advice
affection
agreement
agriculture
airport
allowance
ancestor
ankle
announcer
antagonist
antidote
antiseptic
anxious
appeared
apply
argument
article
artist
ascent
assembly
assistance
assistant
astrology
astronomy
attendance
attendant
attention
attract
attraction
audience
autograph
bandage
beautify
beginning
behave
behaviour
belief
biography
biology
bitumen
blood
boarder
border
bore
borrow
bottle
boundary
breathe
brightness
brilliant
budget
built
burglar
calculator
calendar
cancel
candidate
carriage
cautious
celebrate
chamber
champion
chance
character
cheque
choir
circumference
circumstances
classify
colony
comfortable
competition
construct
contract
contradict
conversation
cooperate
correct
cough
council
counterfeit
courage
culture
curious
curtain
customer
cyclist
dairy
defence
definite
dense
dentist
desire
dessert
determine
diagonal
diagram
dialogue
diameter
direction
disappointed
disease
dissolve
distant
distract
divide
drawer
economic
educate
electorate
electric
emperor
employ
employed
endurance
enemy
enormous
enquiry
entertain
entrance
envelope
environment
equipment
erosion
especially
eventually
examine
exceed
excellent
excessive
executive

A Spelling list

exercise
exhaust
exhibition
experience
experiment
export
expose
extinct
extract
faithful
fertile
fiction
figure
flavour
flight
florist
fluent
fluid
foreign
forth
fortunate
friendship
furious
gaze
genetic
genre
geography
geology
geometry
government
governor
graphic
groceries
guidance
guide
guilt
habit
happiness
harbour
hardship
harvest
haste
heaven
homestead
honour
horizon
horrible
human
humorous
humour
ignorance
imaginary
imagine
immediate
import
impossible
improvement
incident
independent
influence
inhabitant
instruct
instrument
intercept
interesting
interfere
interrupt
interview
introduction
investigate
invisible
jail
jealous
jewellery
judgement
juicy
kneel
knelt
knowledge
labour
laziness
ledge
leisure
library
liquid
machinery
magnificent
majority
manual
manufacture
manuscript
married
marvellous
masculine
mathematics
maximum
mayor
meanwhile
media
messenger
meteor
microbe
microscope
minimum
minister
miserable
mobile
modern
mosquito
musician
mysterious
necessary
neighbour
nuclear
numerous
obstruct
occasion
occasionally
occupation
occupy
occurred
operation
opportunity
opposition
ordinary
original
outcast
outlaw
outlive
outrun
overhead
palace
panic
paragraph
parallel
parcel
parliament
particular
pastime
pastures
patient
percentage
perimeter
periscope
permanent
permission
persist
personal
persuade
pitiful
planet
plaster
plastic

A Spelling list

platform
pleasure
plentiful
populate
population
portable
porter
position
possess
possible
principal
principle
probably
procession
profit
program
prologue
property
prophecy
prosperous
protection
provide
public
publication
publisher
puncture
purchase
purify
purpose
quality
quantity
quarrel
realise
receipt
receive
recent
recipe
recognise
recommend
record
recover
rectangular
refreshment
regards
regular
replied
represent
republic
rescue
restaurant
revenue
rifle
rocket
ruin
savage
science
scientist
scramble
secret
secretary
section
seize
select
senator
sense
sentence
serious
service
several
shadow
shrub
sign
silence
silent
similar
simple
sincerely
soak
solar
soldier
special
spectator
split
spoil
spoken
sprang
square
startle
stationary
stationery
steady
stomach
structure
substance
subtract
succeed
suffer
sufficient
suitable
support
surprise
survivor
sword
telescope
temperature
terrify
theatre
therefore
thoroughly
tight
tongue
tourist
towel
tractor
transport
traveller
truthful
twist
unconscious
underground
undermine
underpay
underweight
underworld
unfortunately
unhealthy
unique
untidy
unusual
useable
vacuum
valuable
variety
various
vast
vehicle
vicious
worship
youth

B Extension spelling list

abandoned
abattoir
abominable
academy
accessory
accompaniment
achieve
acknowledgement
acquittal
admissible
aerial
aggravate
aggression
alibi
allegation
allegiance
allotment
already
aluminium
amiable
anguish
annihilate
antibiotic
appalling
apparent
appreciate
arguably
ascertain
assignment
assimilate
associate
attachment
attitude
bachelor
baptise
basically
beneficial
bequeath
biscuit
bodily
boutique
brigadier
brochure
budgeted
bureaucracy
business
campaign
cancellation
casually
changeable
character
civilian
clientele
coincidence
colleague
commitment
committee
competent
conceited
conference
conscientious
consistency
contemporary
controversial
corroborate
counterfeit
critically
currency
cynical
deceive
defendant
definitely
deliberate
dependant
derelict
desperate
deterred
dilemma
disastrous
discipline
dispensable
dissuade
drastically
dungeon
ecstatic
elaborate
elegance
embarrass
enthusiastically
equivalent
estuary
exasperate
exhilarate
extravagance
fallible
fascinate
feasible
foliage
franchise
frantically
fundamental
fuselage
gauge
ghetto
gimmick
glamour
gossiped
graffiti
grandeur
grievous
grotesque
harass
haughty
hazardous
hindrance
honorary
hygiene
hysterically
identical
imaginary
implement
improvise
inappropriate
incidentally
ingredient
inoculate
inseparable
insistent
installation
instantaneous
interrogation
intrigue
irritable
jeweller
jubilant
karaoke
laboratory
lacquer
latitude
liaise
liquor
longitude
luncheon
luscious
luxury
magnanimous
marriage
martyr
massacre
meagre
miniature
ministry
minuscule

B Extension spelling list

morgue
municipal
mystify
naive
nausea
negotiate
notoriety
nuisance
nutritious
oblique
obscene
offence
opinion
outrageous
overwrought
pageant
paralyse
particularly
peninsula
perennial
perilous
personnel
physically
physique
plague
plausible
preferred
prejudice
prestige
prevalent
privilege
procedure
propaganda
publicly
quarrelled
queue
realm
reconnaissance
recruit
referee
rehearsal
reiterate
rendezvous
repertoire
reservoir
retrieve
rhythmic
sachet
satellite
sceptic
schedule
scourge
segregate
sentinel
siege
silhouette
slaughter
solemn
souvenir
spasm
specifically
spontaneous
squalor
stealth
subtle
succulent
superstitious
surgeon
surveillance
susceptible
suspicious
symbolic
symmetrical
syrup
tarpaulin
technically
technique
temporary
terrestrial
theatre
thorough
throughout
tragedy
treachery
truly
tyranny
unequalled
upheaval
usually
utensil
vaccinate
veneer
vengeance
vigorous
volleys
voluntary
weight
wholly
wield
woollen
woolly
wretched
yacht
zealous
zoology

C Problem words

Some **pairs of endings** can cause confusion. Some common words with these endings are listed below. Study them carefully.

-able and -ible

-able	adorable	amicable	applicable	breakable
	changeable	curable	drinkable	enviable
	excusable	liable	navigable	negotiable
	noticeable	practicable	reliable	serviceable
	usable	valuable	variable	viable
-ible	accessible	audible	collapsible	convertible
	credible	defensible	divisible	edible
	eligible	flexible	forcible	horrible
	illegible	impossible	incredible	indivisible
	inedible	ineligible	inflexible	intelligible
	invincible	invisible	irresistible	legible
	negligible	possible	responsible	sensible
	terrible	unintelligible	visible	

-ance and -ence

-ance	acceptance	acquaintance	admittance	alliance
	allowance	ambulance	annoyance	appearance
	appliance	attendance	avoidance	balance
	brilliance	circumstance	clearance	defiance
	deliverance	disappearance	distance	elegance
	endurance	extravagance	fragrance	guidance
	ignorance	importance	inheritance	instance
	insurance	nuisance	observance	radiance
	reassurance	relevance	resonance	significance
	substance	tolerance		
-ence	adolescence	audience	coincidence	conference
	confidence	congruence	conscience	consequence
	convenience	dependence	difference	diligence
	equivalence	evidence	excellence	existence
	experience	impatience	inexperience	insistence
	licence	magnificence	negligence	obedience
	occurrence	patience	persistence	presence
	reference	resilience	reverence	sequence
	subsidence	subsistence	violence	

C Problem words

-ary and -ery

-ary (nouns)	anniversary centenary itinerary sanctuary vocabulary	aviary dictionary library secretary	boundary estuary missionary summary	burglary glossary salary tributary
-ary (adjectives)	auxiliary extraordinary legendary necessary solitary visionary	contrary hereditary mercenary ordinary supplementary voluntary	customary honorary military rotary unnecessary	disciplinary imaginary monetary secondary veterinary
-ery (nouns)	archery cannery discovery jewellery misery refinery treachery	artery cemetery finery lottery nursery scenery trickery	battery confectionery flattery machinery pottery slavery	bravery delivery gallery mastery recovery stationery

-ous, -ious and -eous

-ous	adventurous carnivorous enormous indigenous monstrous ridiculous wondrous	anonymous conspicuous generous luminous numerous superfluous	autonomous continuous hazardous miraculous poisonous thunderous	callous dangerous impetuous monotonous prosperous treacherous
-ious	amphibious industrious odious	copious luxurious studious	curious melodious victorious	hilarious notorious
-eous	beauteous miscellaneous	courteous nauseous	hideous simultaneous	igneous spontaneous

D Homonyms

Homonyms are words that sound alike but are spelt differently. Check the pairs and groups in this section.

air heir	The **air** was fresh and clear. The prince was **heir** to the throne.
allowed aloud	She was **allowed** to go. They read the book **aloud**.
ate eight	The boy **ate** the cake. She had **eight** books.
bail bale	They will **bail** water out of the boat. There is the **bale** of wool.
bare bear	His **bare** back was burnt by the sun. She could not **bear** to leave the dog.
bean been	The **bean** crop was very good. He has **been** to the circus.
berry bury	The **berry** was on top of the ice cream. They will **bury** the treasure.
bight bite	Fishermen brave the dangers of the Great Australian **Bight**. The dog will **bite** the other animal.
blew blue	The wind **blew** strongly. The shirt was a **blue** colour.
boy buoy	Did you see the **boy**? The **buoy** was floating near the rocks.
brake break	The **brake** on the bike did not work. Did he **break** the ruler?
bread bred	They ate several slices of **bread**. The lions were **bred** in the zoo.
buy by bye	We will **buy** the present. He walked **by** the river. She will bid her friend good-**bye**.
ceiling sealing	They painted the **ceiling** in the kitchen. The men were **sealing** up the old mine.
cent scent sent	He did not have a **cent**. The tracker dog followed the **scent**. She was **sent** away.
cereal serial	They had a bowl of **cereal**. I wrote down the **serial** numbers of the notes.
check cheque	Did you **check** the work? They wrote out a **cheque** for the goods.
chews choose	The animal **chews** on the bone. Will you **choose** a new book?
creak creek	The old timbers will **creak**. They went to the **creek**.
currant current	The **currant** loaf was eaten. There was a strong **current** in the creek.
dear deer	It was his **dear** friend. The **deer** was in the paddock.
desert dessert	They travelled into the **desert**. What will we have for **dessert**?
dew due	The **dew** was on the grass. The money is **due** to be paid today.

D Homonyms

die	Many people **die** in wartime.
dye	The red **dye** was very bright.
fair	She has **fair** hair.
fare	The **fare** on the bus was one dollar.
feat	Crossing the desert was a great **feat**.
feet	His **feet** were sore after the long run.
find	They could not **find** the money.
fined	The motorist was **fined** for speeding.
fir	This is a fine **fir** tree.
fur	The animal had grey **fur**.
flour	The **flour** was used to make a cake.
flower	He worked in the **flower** garden.
for	She went **for** a walk.
four	There are **four** people at the shop.
foul	It was a **foul** smell.
fowl	The **fowl** was put in the chicken shed.
grate	The **grate** was made of iron.
great	This is a **great** book.
groan	I heard the **groan** of the injured pedestrian.
grown	She had **grown** a lot since last year.
guessed	He **guessed** the answer.
guest	She was a **guest** in the house.
hall	They danced in the **hall**.
haul	It was a large **haul** of fish.
heal	The wound will **heal**.
heel	The runner's left **heel** was blistered.
hear	Did you **hear** the sound?
here	Come **here** at once!
heard	I **heard** the sound.
herd	There is the **herd** of cattle.
higher	This is **higher** than the ladder.
hire	Will you **hire** a car?
him	I saw **him** at the gate.
hymn	They sang a **hymn** at the service.
hoarse	The child was **hoarse** from shouting.
horse	The **horse** is in the paddock.
hole	There is a **hole** in the fence.
whole	Do not eat the **whole** cake.
hour	Meet me in one **hour**.
our	This is **our** new car.
knew	I **knew** the answer.
new	Where is the **new** boat?
knot	Tie the **knot** carefully.
not	She is **not** coming to the party.
know	He does not **know** where the car is.
no	She has **no** money.
knows	The boy **knows** the answer.
nose	The player injured his **nose**.
lead	The **lead** pipe is brand new.
led	They **led** the horse into the paddock.

D Homonyms

loan	He had a **loan** of his friend's bike.
lone	The **lone** animal grazed in the field.
mail	She collected the **mail**.
male	A **male** tiger was in the ring.
main	They went along the **main** road.
mane	The lion had a golden **mane**.
meat	They bought some **meat** for dinner.
meet	The girl will **meet** her at the bridge.
mind	She did not **mind** the noise.
mined	The workers **mined** for coal.
missed	The arrow **missed** the target.
mist	They could not see through the **mist**.
one	**One** of the horses is missing.
won	The young girl easily **won** the race.
pail	They carried a large **pail** of water.
pale	She had a **pale** face.
pain	The **pain** in his injured arm was severe.
pane	The ball broke the **pane** of glass.
passed	She **passed** the slow moving vehicle.
past	I walked **past** the yard.
pause	There was a **pause** in the news broadcast.
paws	The kitten has tiny **paws**.
paw	The dog had an injured **paw**.
poor	The woman was in **poor** health.
pour	**Pour** out the milk.
peace	Late in the year **peace** was declared.
piece	Have a **piece** of cake.
plain	The animals wandered onto the **plain**.
plane	The **plane** landed in the swamp.
rain	The **rain** poured down.
reign	The country was settled in the **reign** of George III.
rein	Take the horse's **rein** please.
real	This diamond is **real**.
reel	He took his fishing **reel** with him.
right	This is the **right** time to finish it.
write	Can he **write** the book?
road	The car travelled down the **road**.
rode	She **rode** the pony at the show.
sail	Can you **sail** this boat?
sale	The **sale** was on at the shopping centre.
saw	I **saw** the new sports car.
sore	The boy had a **sore** arm.
scene	It was a **scene** of great beauty.
seen	Have you **seen** the lost dog?
sea	The **sea** was very calm.
see	Can you **see** that small shrub?
sew	They will **sew** the cloth.
so	It was **so** heavy he could not lift it.
sow	The farmer will **sow** the seed.
some	They had **some** cake.
sum	She has a large **sum** of money.

D Homonyms

stair	Climb that **stair** please.
stare	Do not **stare** at those people.
steal	They should not **steal** the money.
steel	She found the **steel** bar.
tail	The small pony has a long **tail**.
tale	They were told an interesting **tale**.
their	I saw **their** house.
there	**There** are many books on the shelves.
they're	**They're** going to the movies.
threw	She **threw** the ball at the fence.
through	The horse galloped **through** the scrub.
tide	The **tide** came in at six o'clock.
tied	The ship was **tied** up at the wharf.
to	I went **to** the shop.
too	Sam went **too**.
two	We bought **two** drinks.
waist	The belt was around her **waist**.
waste	They did not **waste** any food.
wait	Perry will **wait** at the gate.
weight	The box was 10 kilograms in **weight**.
war	The **war** was over at the end of the year.
wore	She **wore** a pretty red dress.
warn	Did you **warn** them about the fire?
worn	His shoes were nearly **worn** out.
weak	The string was very **weak**.
week	They will go home in a **week**.
weather	I do not like this cold **weather**.
whether	She does not know **whether** or not to leave.
which	Do you know **which** book to study?
witch	The **witch** was a character in the story.
who's	**Who's** going to the movies?
whose	I do not know **whose** book this is.
wood	The **wood** in the corner was rotting.
would	She **would** not finish the work.

E Confusing pairs of words

Word	Meaning	Example
accept except	take something not including	They will **accept** the present. All **except** Tom went to the zoo.
advice advise	information (noun) provide information (verb)	She gave me good **advice**. He will **advise** his brother of the problem.
aisle isle	a corridor short name for island	The bride walked down the **aisle**. There is the **isle** of pines.
alley ally	narrow street one on your side	They searched along the **alley**. His brother was his **ally**.
altar alter	sacred table in church change	The couple knelt at the **altar**. They will **alter** the answer.
bridal bridle	relating to a bride part of harness for horse	The **bridal** party arrived in white cars. The **bridle** is on the horse.
collage college	picture made with glue place for education	The artist finished the **collage**. They went to **college** in the city.
complement compliment	that which completes something words of praise	Red **complements** the house. She paid him a **compliment**.
confidant confident	one a person trusts sure of oneself	His **confidant** was his younger brother. They were **confident** they would win.
council counsel	local government group advice	The **council** made a decision. He asked his teacher's **counsel**.
dairy diary	place for milking cows written record	She saw cheese being made at the **dairy**. He wrote in his **diary** every day.
draft draught	rough first attempt flow of air	She corrected her first **draft**. Do not sit in the **draught**.
eligible illegible	suitable not able to be read	John was **eligible** to play in the team. His writing was **illegible**.
ensure insure	make sure money to cover loss	Mark will **ensure** he finishes the work. They will **insure** their art collection.
flair flare	talent or ability sudden bright light	She has a **flair** for theatrical work. The rescue **flare** lit up the sky.
gild guild	cover with gold a group or company	They will **gild** the metal rings. At the **guild** meeting many work issues were discussed.
gilt guilt	gold material shame or wrong doing	The **gilt** on the frame had peeled away. The **guilt** of the criminal was quite clear.
hangar hanger	shed for aircraft used to hang clothes	The Cessna was in the new **hangar**. All the **hangers** were in the wardrobe.
human humane	man, woman or child preventing suffering	Each **human** was allocated a ration of food. The vet always treated the animals in a **humane** way.
later latter	next in time the last mentioned	She left the party **later** than her brother. Of the foods meat and fish, I prefer the **latter**.
lightening lightning	to make lighter flash of electrical light	They were **lightening** the load. The **lightning** flashed across the sky.
metal mettle	hard substance courage	The scrap **metal** was on the truck. The young soldiers showed their **mettle** in the first conflict.

E Confusing pairs of words

Word	Meaning	Example
miner	mine worker	The **miner** was working at a great depth.
minor	one who is not legally an adult	This product cannot be sold to **minors**.
moral	meaning behind a story	The **moral** of the story could easily be discovered.
morale	confidence	The **morale** of the winning team was very high.
passed	went ahead (verb)	The car **passed** the petrol tanker.
past	further along (preposition)	All of them walked **past** the shop.
practice	repeating something (noun)	Did you go to netball **practice**?
practise	doing something over and over (verb)	She will **practise** the piano.
precede	to go before someone or something	The band will **precede** the marchers.
proceed	to go forward	Do not **proceed** past this point.
principal	head person	The **principal** interviewed the children.
principle	general rule	The man studied the **principles** of aerodynamics.
stationary	not moving	The cars in the traffic jam were **stationary** for an hour.
stationery	office equipment	The paper was in the **stationery** cupboard.
storey	floor or level of building	This building is ten **storeys** high.
story	tale or account	The **story** he read was quite interesting.
straight	not bent	She drew a **straight** line on the book.
strait	stretch of water	The boat crossed the narrow **strait**.
trail	path	They left the **trail** to search for the dog.
trial	case in court	The **trial** will be held next week.
wander	to walk away	They will **wander** across the field.
wonder	to think about	She **wondered** where it was hidden.

F Contractions

Contractions are the **abbreviated forms** of two words. The position of the **missing letter** is indicated by an **apostrophe** (e.g. *I'm = I am*).

Contractions with *not*

could not	➡	couldn't
did not	➡	didn't
do not	➡	don't
does not	➡	doesn't
had not	➡	hadn't
have not	➡	haven't
shall not	➡	shan't
should not	➡	shouldn't
was not	➡	wasn't
will not	➡	won't
were not	➡	weren't
would not	➡	wouldn't

Contractions with *is*

he is	➡	he's
it is	➡	it's
she is	➡	she's
that is	➡	that's
there is	➡	there's
what is	➡	what's
where is	➡	where's
who is	➡	who's

Contractions with *are*

we are	➡	we're
you are	➡	you're
they are	➡	they're

Contractions with *will*

I will	➡	I'll
you will	➡	you'll
he will	➡	he'll
she will	➡	she'll
they will	➡	they'll

Contractions with *had or would*

I had (would)	➡	I'd
you had (would)	➡	you'd
he had (would)	➡	he'd
she had (would)	➡	she'd
we had (would)	➡	we'd
they had (would)	➡	they'd

Contractions with *have*

I have	➡	I've
you have	➡	you've
we have	➡	we've
they have	➡	they've

G American English

Americans use different words from Australians for a number of common things.

Australian English	American English
autumn	fall
barbecue	cookout
biscuit	cookie
bonnet (car)	hood
boot (car)	trunk
brumby	mustang
bulb	globe
bumper bar	fender
car	auto
caravan	trailer
chemist's shop	drugstore
footpath	sidewalk
frying pan	skillet
garbage bin	trash can
jam	jelly
lollies	candy
pavement	sidewalk
petrol	gas
pig	hog
post code	zip code
power point	outlet
puncture	flat
railway	railroad
rubbish	trash
soft drink	soda
station	ranch
stockyard	corral
tap	faucet
timber	lumber
torch	flashlight
tram	streetcar
waistcoat	vest

H Latin roots

ago actus **I do**

act	action	active	actor	actual
agency	agent	agile	inaction	inactive
react	transact	transaction		

anima **life, breath, soul**

animal	animate	inanimate

annus **a year**

anniversary	annual	biannual	biennial
perennial	superannuation	triennial	

cado casus **I fall**

accident	cascade	casual	casualty
decay	deciduous	incident	occasion

capio captus **I take**

accept	anticipate	capable	captive
captor	capture	except	intercept
participate	receive	receiver	

caput capitis **head**

cape	capital	captain	chief
decapitate	precipice		

cedo cessus **I go**

ancestor	antecedent	cease	exceed	intercede
precede	predecessor	proceed	process	procession
recede	succeed	successful	unsuccessful	

cito **I rouse**

excite	excitement	exciting	recitation
recite	resuscitate	resuscitation	

colo cultus **I till**

agricultural	agriculture	colonise	colony	cultivate
cultivation	cultural	culture	horticulture	uncultivated

cor cordis **heart**

cordial	cordially	core	courage
courageous	discourage	encourage	

curro cursus **I run**

courier	course	courser	coursing	currency
current	excursion	occur	occurrence	recur

decem **ten**

December	decimal

H Latin roots

dens dentis **tooth**

dental	dentist	dentistry	indent	trident

dico dictus **I say**

benediction	contradict	contradiction	dictate	dictation
dictator	diction	dictionary	predict	verdict

duco ductus **I lead**

abduct	abduction	aqueduct	conduct	conductor
deduct	education	educational	educator	introduce
introduction	produce	product	production	reduce
reduction				

facio factus **I make**

affection	affectionate	artificial	benefactor	beneficial
benefit	counterfeit	defeat	effect	efficient
fact	factor	factory	magnificent	magnify
manufacture	perfect	sacrifice	satisfaction	satisfactory
significant	signify			

finis **end**

confine	define	definite	definition
final	finale	finish	finite
infinite	refine	refined	unfinished

fortis **strong**

comfort	comfortable	effort	enforce	force
forceful	forcible	fort	fortification	fortify
fortitude	fortress	reinforce	uncomfortable	unfortified

jacio jactus **I throw**

adjective	dejected	eject	inject
injection	interject	object	objector
project	projector	reject	subject

lego lectus **I read, gather, choose**

collect	collection	collector	diligent	elect
election	elector	eligible	illegible	intellect
intelligence	lecture	lecturer	legend	legible
neglect	recollect	select	selection	

locus **place**

dislocate	local	locality	locate
location	locomotive		

magnus **great**

magnificent	magnify	magnitude

manus **hand**

manacle	manage	manager	manual
manufacture	manufacturer	manuscript	

H Latin roots

memor **mindful**

commemorate	memento	memoirs	memorable	memorandum
memorial	memorise	memory	remember	remembrance

mens mentis **mind**

demented	mental	mentality	mentally

minor **small**

minor	minority

multus **many**

multiple	multiplication	multiply	multitude

pono positus **I place**

compose	composer	composition	compound	depose
deposit	depot	dispose	expose	impose
impostor	opponent	oppose	opposite	opposition
pose	position	positive	post	postage
postpone	posture	proposal	propose	purpose
suppose				

populus **people**

populace	popular	popularity	populate	population
populous	public	publicity	republic	

porto **I carry**

deport	export	exporter	import	importance
important	importer	portable	porter	report
reporter	support	transport	transportation	

puto **I think**

compute	computer	dispute	disreputable
reputable	reputation		

rego rectus **I rule**

correct	correction	direct	direction	director
erect	incorrect	irregular	rectify	regent
regiment	region	regular	regulate	

rumpo ruptus **I break**

abrupt	abruptly	bankrupt	corrupt	corruption
disrupt	erupt	eruption	interrupt	interruption

sentio sensus **I feel**

consent	nonsense	resent	sensation	sense
sensible	sensitive	sentence	sentiment	

H Latin roots

struo structus **I build**

construct, construction, constructive, destroy, destroyer
destruction, destructive, indestructible, instruct, instruction
instructor, obstruct, obstruction, structure

tendo tensus **I stretch**

attend, attendance, attention, attentive, contend
contender, distend, extend, extension, extensive
intend, intense, pretence, pretend, superintend
superintendent, tense, tension

teneo tentus **I hold**

abstain, contain, contents, continent, continue
continuous, detain, entertain, entertainer, entertainment
maintain, obtain, retain, sustain, tenacious
tenacity, tenant

traho tractus **I draw**

attract, attraction, attractive, betray, contract
contraction, contractor, extract, portrait, portray
retreat, subtract, subtraction, trace, tractor

venio ventus **I come**

adventure, adventurer, adventurous, avenue, convene
convenient, convent, convention, event, eventful
intervene, invent, invention, inventive, inventor
prevent, prevention, revenue

verto versus **I turn**

adversary, advertise, advertisement, anniversary, conversation
converse, convert, divert, invert, reverse
universal, universe, university, vertex, vertical

video visus **I see**

advice, advise, evidence, evident, invisible
provide, provision, review, revise, supervise
survey, surveyor, view, visible, vision
visit, visitor, visual

I Greek roots

arche **rule**

anarchy	monarchy	oligarchy		

aster **a star**

aster	asterisk	astrology	astronomical	astronomy

baros **weight**

barometer	isobar			

bios **life**

amphibious	autobiography	biography	biology	microbe

chronos **time**

chronicle	chronometer	synchronisation		

demos **the people**

democracy	democrat	democratic	epidemic	

ge **the earth**

geography	geologist	geology	geometrical	geometry

grapho **I write**

autobiography	autograph	biography	geography	graphic
graphite	paragraph	stenographer	telegraph	

logos **speech, discourse**

apology	catalogue	dialogue	epilogue	

metron **measure**

barometer	chronometer	diameter	gasometer	geometry
meter	metre	metric	micrometer	perimeter
symmetry	thermometer			

micros **small**

microbe	microfilm	micron	microscopic	

pathos **feeling**

apathy	empathy	pathetic	sympathy	

phone **sound**

megaphone	microphone	phonics	radiophone	
symphony	telephone			

phos **light**

phosphorus	photograph	photographer	photography	

polis **city**

cosmopolitan	metropolitan	political	politics	

I Greek roots

polys **many**

polygamy	polygon		

scopeo **I view**

microscope	periscope	telescopic	

tele **distant, afar**

telegram	telegraph	telepathy	telephone
telescope	television		

therme **heat**

isotherm	thermal	thermometer	

zoon **animal**

zoo	zoological	zoologist	zoology

Answers

1 Basic sounds: vowels and consonants

Page 1

1 back, camp, glad, gram, stand, thank, that

2 eighteen, bait, plain, today, brain, stay, plate

3 space L, display L, graze L, apple S, brave L, became L, taken L, spray L, shady L

4 L: lazy, train, game, take, navy, swayed, named. S: arrow, among

5 (Sample answers) Bat: cat, rat, sat. Cake: lake, bake, rake, take. Rain: brain, stain, train. Pay: bay, lay, stay

Page 2

1 help, seven, tread, jetty, fresh, chest, slept, setting

2 lady, three, seat, monkey, relief, beetle, greeting

3 west, best, test, rest, vest, zest

4 deed, feed, heed, need, seed, bleed, freed, steed

5 L: screen, grief, donkey, leave, needle, nearly, field. S: press, ready

6 (Sample answers) Eat: beat, neat, seat, cheat. Baby: lady, shady, lazy. Chief: thief, relief, grief. Free: tree, glee, three

Page 3

1 gift, still, spring, little, winter, silver, middle

2 shine, strike, while, flies, tried, sty, sighted, frighten

3 decide L, smile L, sight L, inside L, tried L, winner S, shine L, frighten L, slick S

4 (Sample answers) Pie: lie, die, vie. Cry: sty, dye, why, fry. Light: bight, sight, tight. Still: bill, fill, chill

5 **a** strike L **b** ivory L **c** admire L **d** fifth S **e** sight L **f** reply L

Page 4

1 ponds, logger, cot, locks, washed, wanted, mopping

2 below, coast, float, shallow, hotel, follow, toast, coach

3 **a** bow, low, sow, tow, blow, flow, grow, slow, snow **b** boat, goat, moat, gloat, float, bloat, throat

4 shadow L, polite S, obey L, radio L, tomato L, ocean L, soldier L, toe L, stroke L

5 (Sample answers) slow L, rode L, oven S, tore L, yellow L, drove L

Page 5

1 such, summer, bunch, trunk, uncle, sunny, hunter, number

2 grew, soon, shoot, rude, stoop, emu, suited, music, stew

3 **a** few, hew, new, pew, blew, crew, slew, stew **b** boon, noon, soon, croon, spoon

4 lute L, crooner L, huge L, supper S, double S, nut S, zebu L, overdo L, enough S

5 **a** sooner L **b** supply S **c** thunder S

Page 6 How much do you know?

1 batch, crash, spread, clog, west, black, awful, finger, check, bullet, stir, push, strong, dance, jetty, tread, sob

2 mapping S, handed S, caravan S, manager S, plate L, straight L, railway L, paddock S

3 sweating S, deadly S, equal L, scheme L, there's S, either L, peaceful L, tennis S

4 Long: seaside, knife, arrive, quite. Short: hilltop, fishy, until, middle, family, fifth

5 (Sample answers) stocking, narrower, dropped, coaches, sorrier, spoken

6 duckling S, couple S, young S, cushion L, parachute L, muddle S, circus S, truthful L

Page 7

1 Hard: calves, camp, copper, costume, canyon, cashew, canoe, coconut, coins, cavern (all other words soft)

2 Hard: games, gauze, giggle, girth, garden, garbage, gases, giddy, gallop, gargle, galaxy

3 (Sample answers) catapult, citizen, distant, funnier, gazebo, jangle, cattery, casual, dispose, cotton, joking, gadget, kidding, lighter, misery, nothing, possible, rifle, satin, totally, visitor, taken, zebra, yodel

Answers

Page 8

1 laughter, hard, liar, surveyor, teacher, about, fork, loiter, lurching, drawn, crowd, porch, hound

2 pounce, record, disturb, squirt, worst, allow, straw, hoist, messenger

3 sound, storm, burnt, first, world, birth, burst, ground, worst, dirty, nurse, sprout, torn, crawl, point, start, sailor, beginner, party, hardship, march, hoist

Page 9

1 **a** blade **b** broom **c** climb **d** crest **e** drive **f** flock **g** front **h** glare **i** group **j** plant

2 **a** prompt, prowl **b** scamp, scoop **c** scrub, screech **d** skate, skipper **e** slack, slope
f smile, small **g** snack, sneer **h** spend, speck **i** split, splay **j** spring, sprout **k** stale, storm **l** stride, string **m** swept, swish **n** thrust, throat

3 (Sample answers) **a** sway, swan, swim **b** sky, skate, skit **c** blow, blew, bleak **d** clay, clap, clatter **e** flat, fling, flap **f** bray, bread, bring **g** cream, crate, cringe **h** drew, drake, drab

Page 10

1 **a** lunch **b** rock **c** correct **d** tuft **e** gulp **f** dump **g** sand **h** long **i** blank **j** blunt

2 (Sample answers) **a** nt: sent, cent, lent **b** pt: crept, kept, wept **c** lt: bolt, gilt, spilt **d** le: battle, rattle, saddle **e** sk: bask, desk, cask **f** st: west, test, most **g** th: south, mouth, north **h** gh: rough, enough, cough

3 **a** stamp **b** much **c** lift **d** vault **e** string **f** trunk **g** crept **h** cast **i** truth **j** rough

Page 11 How much do you know?

1 (Sample answers) below, dazzle, forced, dazed, hidden, jewel, koala, linger, basked, needle, pebble, beach, satin, tomato, vacant, waiting, bowl, zoned

2 (Sample answers) **a** save **b** zip **c** lame **d** dent **e** line **f** pole

3 **a** scorch **b** drought **c** window **d** chirp **e** drawing

4 **a** spilling, spire, spoiling **b** grinned, greatly, gristle **c** climber, cleanser, clench **d** sweater, swimmer, swampy **e** flannel, flavour, fleecy **f** bracket, branches, breathe

5 **a** clump **b** basket **c** elect **d** script **e** gulping **f** shifted

Pages 12–13 Review test 1

1 Long: shape, Sunday, always, grateful, believe, scene, sheep, equal. Short: voyage, average, attend, crack, dentist, family, admire, educate

2 fend, lend, mend, tend, trend, spend, pretend

3 meat, seat, neat, bleat, pleat, treat

4 (Sample answers) **a** cold, bold, told, scold **b** boat, moat, float, goat

5 adult S, funny S, gullies S, ruler L, during L, fortune L, injury L, rubbish S, uncles S

6 **a** seizing L **b** item L **c** coastal L **d** statue L **e** hearty S

7 Hard: corncob, gazebo, gamble, consumer, gasket, gangster, corridor, coast, gargle, cover (all other words soft)

8 (Sample answers) teaching, burial, moisture, worrier, honesty, canteen, dazed, witness, general, junior, survey, keenly, paused, ransom, toughen

9 (Sample answers) lowest, sprawl, circle, suburb, hardship, worse, person, calves, towel, murmur, growth

10 (Sample answers) **a** spin, spray, spot, span **b** stop, stray, steady, steed **c** flee, flat, flare, flake **d** trap, trip, try, trike **e** two, tweed, tweak, twine

11 **a** swept **b** stump **c** result **d** silken **e** suspect **f** frost

12 **a** bent, lent, sent, spent **b** rank, link, pink, blink **c** pump, sump, thump, dump

Answers

Page 14 Puzzle time 1

Crossword 1

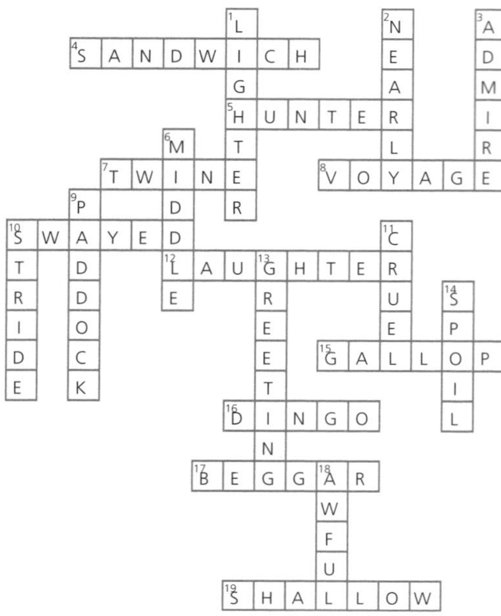

Wordsearch 1

Words: wanted, family, brain, hawk, silver, gases, needle, couple, coach, movie

2 Spelling strategies

Page 15

1 **a** hand, lank **b** lips, taps **c** drink, lunch **d** loose, teams **e** mouth, earth

2 making, eatery; dream, hears; often, after; depart, depend; wooden, mantis; steam, alone; castles, smother; window, winter

3 (Sample answers) **a** sorry, worry **b** claws, above **c** item, clan **d** given, yours **e** evens, cress **f** braid, brush

Quick check

1 F **2** T **3** T **4** F **5** F **6** F **7** F **8** F

Page 16

1 **a** match, valet **b** wedding, yelling **c** sister, cooler **d** whole, while **e** about, short **f** stick, start

2 smoke, smile; dishes, lashes; closing, shoving; putting, jotting; cannot, carrot; evening, morning; nurse, never; hammer, dinner

3 (Sample answers) **a** farrier, dimmer **b** sitting, willing **c** bunch, lurch **d** decide, reside

Quick check

1 T **2** F **3** T **4** F **5** T **6** F **7** T **8** F

Page 17

1 **a** lie, be **b** shall, low **c** care, less, are **d** ear, wear **e** favour, it **f** eat **g** port, import, ant **h** broad, cast, road **i** eat, her **j** tea

2 **a** list **b** tin **c** ten **d** owe **e** tea **f** own **g** hall **h** row **i** ear **j** and

3 **a** particle **b** therefore **c** excellent **d** irrigate **e** furnish **f** shading **g** steel **h** shallow **i** attention **j** startle

Quick check

1 boarder **2** sentences **3** fairies **4** dreary **5** dashing **6** mourn **7** performer **8** leased

Page 18

1 **a** ark **b** choose **c** dew **d** bite **e** deer **f** bred **g** fined **h** bass **i** feet **j** sell **k** creek **l** bow **m** carrot **n** cruise **o** eight **p** fare **q** fowl **r** blue **s** claws **t** dye **u** bawl **v** fourth **w** grown **x** birth

Answers

2 **a** buy **b** cheap **c** coral **d** boarder **e** beech **f** been **g** bale **h** break **i** cellar **j** earn

3 **a** draught **b** use **c** fete **d** floor **e** phrase **f** freeze **g** gnaw **h** grate **i** guessed **j** hare

Page 19

1 **a** heel **b** raise **c** seas **d** sought **e** idol **f** wore **g** poll **h** would **i** witch **j** lone **k** tied **l** prays **m** won **n** thrown **o** lute **p** sighed **q** sweet **r** hymn **s** towed **t** pier **u** there **v** lane **w** whale **x** mist

2 **a** bore **b** grater **c** mail **d** made **e** paced **f** pale **g** buoy **h** current **i** hail **j** lead

3 **a** prize **b** peddle **c** seam **d** rode **e** steak **f** wade **g** weight **h** strait **i** write **j** rein

Page 20

1 **a** fair **b** fair **c** bank **d** bank **e** calf **f** calf **g** ground **h** ground **i** match **j** match **k** prune **l** prune **m** ring **n** ring **o** fast **p** fast **q** form **r** form

2 **a** case **b** drill **c** mean **d** crop **e** perch **f** grain **g** hide **h** lean **i** felt **j** light

Page 21

1 **a** an animal **b** a machine **c** a bird **d** a penalty **e** substance for road building **f** group of mountains **g** pause in work **h** used in map making **i** an animal **j** to coach

2 **a** sign **b** sign **c** stock **d** stock **e** suit **f** suit **g** grate **h** grate **i** club **j** club

3 **a** beak of bird, an account **b** to wish for, not short **c** king or queen, instrument for measuring **d** stone, cause disturbance **e** short period of time, put letters together to make words

Page 22 How much do you know?

1 **a** F **b** F **c** T **d** F **e** T **f** F **g** T **h** T

2 **a** T **b** T **c** T **d** T **e** F **f** T

3 **a** climate **b** bower **c** against **d** allotment **e** locate **f** pirate **g** sinking **h** targeting

4 **a** lapse **b** maid **c** pale **d** peddle **e** poll **f** prays **g** stair **h** tax **i** threw **j** veil

5 **a** wrapped **b** tow **c** isle **d** bowled **e** serial **f** sight **g** flee **h** soul

6 **a** file **b** spoke **c** hail **d** row **e** cross **f** park

Page 23

1 **a** breathe, breathes, breathed, breathing, breathless
b grazes, grazed, grazing, grazier
c inspects, inspected, inspecting, inspection, inspector

2 **a** **i** preparations **ii** preparatory
b **i** strangely **ii** strangest
c **i** divisible **ii** division

Page 24

1 **a** tastes, tasted, tasting, tastily, tasteful, distasteful **b** eases, eased, easing, easily, uneasily **c** supplies, supplied, supplying, supplier, resupplies, resupplied, resupplying

2 **a** **i** settlement **ii** resettle **b** **i** attraction **ii** attractively

3 **a** departure, department
b employee, employer, employment, unemployment
c completion

Page 25

1 **a** numeracy **b** tapestries **c** worshipping **d** impassable **e** tolerable **f** windcheater **g** scorekeeper **h** expendable

2 **a** deformed **b** deflated **c** decently **d** definite **e** delightful **f** depression **g** deleting **h** departure

Answers

3 **a** re, resigned **b** pon, ponderous **c** re, reaction **d** can, vacancy **e** joy, overjoyed **f** der, tenderise **g** ob, objector **h** fer, preference **i** form, performance

4 **a** gelignite **b** turpentine **c** environment **d** disorder **e** sympathy **f** monitor **g** located **h** sentiment

Page 26

1 dismal, unhappy; abruptly, suddenly; display, show; bought, purchased; burglary, theft; broad, wide; conceal, hide; absurd, ridiculous; brutal, cruel; applaud, clap

2 **a** adhere **b** commence **c** astonish **d** earnings **e** obvious **f** courteous **g** clumsy **h** immense

3 **a** holiday **b** taste **c** careful **d** valuable **e** freedom **f** build **g** student **h** sincere **i** prohibit **j** strange **k** often **l** solemn

Page 27

1 reveal, disclose; notify, advise; extensive, large; obstruct, hinder; lively, vigorous; holy, sacred; molten, melted; dangerous, perilous; remember, recollect; shake, tremble

2 **a** wealthy **b** adorned **c** likeness **d** affectionate **e** preserve **f** immense

3 **a** spectator **b** narrative **c** mysterious **d** friend **e** movement **f** foretell **g** amusement **h** fragment **i** funny **j** necessary **k** weariness **l** compelled

Page 28

1 imports, exports; mourn, rejoice; cruelty, kindness; inferior, superior; briskly, slowly; valuable, worthless; wealthy, poor; conceal, reveal; beneath, above; broad, narrow

2 **a** careless **b** small **c** descend **d** rural **e** brilliant **f** industrious **g** allow **h** expensive

3 **a** weaken **b** negative **c** vertical **d** presence **e** natural **f** finish **g** cheerful **h** increase **i** slowly **j** fierce **k** strange **l** hate

Page 29

1 **a** scarcity **b** disperse **c** graceful **d** inactive **e** defeat **f** mobile **g** recollect **h** beginning **i** minimum **j** small **k** collect **l** foolish **m** majority **n** comedy **o** important **p** barren

2 **a** present **b** destruction **c** ascent **d** ashore **e** subtraction **f** unearthed **g** internal **h** rude

3 **a** frequently **b** boring **c** repulsion **d** temporary **e** friendship **f** serious **g** amateur **h** changeable **i** lazy **j** transparent **k** contraction **l** sensible

Page 30

1 **a** disadvantage **b** disallow **c** disappear **d** disapprove **e** discontent **f** discontinue **g** dislike **h** disobedient **i** disobey **j** disorganise

2 **a** unaware **b** unselfish **c** unskilful **d** unclothe **e** insane **f** inaudible **g** incorrect **h** unhappy **i** unfaithful **j** unnecessary

3 **a** irreligious **b** misbehave **c** impatient **d** misfortune **e** impure **f** misrepresent **g** immature **h** illegal **i** misunderstand **j** irregular **k** immortal **l** illegible

4 **a** disbelieve **b** decentralise **c** disconnect **d** unworthy **e** mistrust **f** irreverent **g** impolite **h** displease **i** disorder **j** immovable **k** inconvenient **l** ungrateful **m** dishonest **n** illogical

Page 31 How much do you know?

1 unreasonable, reasonably

2 courageous, courageously, encourage, encourages, encouraged, encouraging

3 **a** revolting **b** listlessness **c** polisher **d** misinform

4 **a** wasteful **b** announce **c** obstinate **d** onlooker

5 **a** dissent **b** attractive **c** brutal **d** extinguish **e** compulsory **f** increase **g** succeed **h** innocence

6 **a** dispossess **b** uncomfortable **c** unsafe **d** misunderstand **e** disengage **f** imperfect **g** disprove **h** unsatisfactory **i** impolite **j** inaudible

Answers

Page 32

1 **a** before **b** before **c** after **d** after **e** after **f** after

2 **a** aloud **b** burial **c** clank

3 **a** actual, advice, agate, alike, amber **b** ease, effort, endure, errand, excite

4 **a** T **b** F **c** T **d** F

5 **a** agile **b** burrow **c** cricket

6 (Sample answers) **a** wool from sheep **b** long narrow cut **c** a flower **d** to mimic or copy **e** story from long ago

7 **a** 13 **b** 13 **c** 12 **d** 10 **e** 14 **f** 12

Page 33

1 **a** huddle **b** impress **c** launch **d** migrant **e** notable

2 **a** after **b** before **c** after **d** after **e** before **f** before

3 **a** narrate, natural, nautical, notion **b** penguin, peninsula, pension, pensive **c** quality, qualm, quantity, quarry

4 (Sample answers) **a** return **b** sandal **c** thief **d** verse

5 **a** dainty **b** declare **c** dread **d** scimitar **e** sepulchre **f** sojourn

6 (Sample answers) **a** pile of stones **b** of great hardship **c** memorial **d** speech spoken by a single person on stage **e** illustration facing the title page in a book

Pages 34–35 Review test 2

1 **a** F **b** F **c** T **d** T **e** F **f** F

2 sword, annul; trick, drawl; merrily, variety; scroll, smooth; marked, rocket; torture, perform

3 conviction, jealousy, reactivate, pardonable, formality, neighbourhood, enrichment, definite

4 **a** bawled **b** bark **c** fur **d** check **e** kerb **f** prays **g** which **h** tale

5 **a** stern **b** stern **c** litter **d** litter **e** firm **f** firm **g** vault **h** vault

6 forces, forced, forcing, forceful, forcefully, enforce, enforces, enforced, enforcing

7 unprepared, preparation

8 **a** ial, specialist **b** wor, worshipped **c** pro, protector **d** ship, leadership **e** fid, fidgeting **f** com, decompose

9 **a** occur **b** sickness **c** terrible **d** jealous **e** damage **f** inhabit **g** entertain **h** rapidly

10 **a** repair **b** reward **c** present **d** worthless **e** impatient **f** cruel

11 **a** 60 **b** 60 **c** 59 **d** 59 **e** 61 **f** 62

Page 36 Puzzle time 2

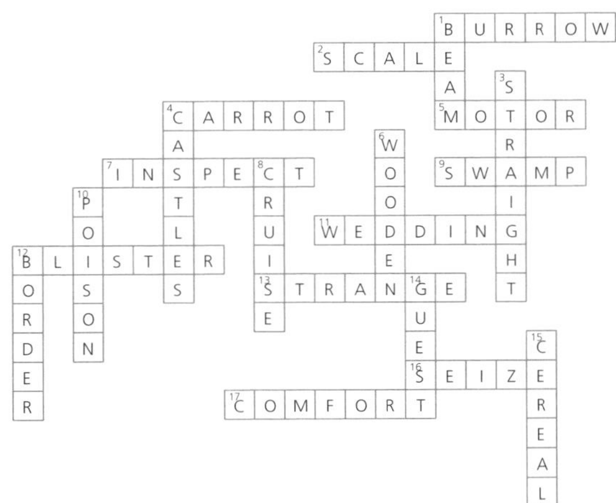

Crossword 2

Wordsearch 2

Words: assist, boarder, seller, ring, fine, rapped, steam, closing, grater, smother

Y	Z	C	M	L	W	H	R	B	X	S	Y	O	L	M
H	Y	G	R	D	U	I	S	S	O	P	S	B	S	X
K	I	G	D	N	I	H	M	T	O	W	E	H	Q	P
B	X	Q	B	R	T	T	P	E	G	B	Y	P	Y	N
B	B	K	A	K	S	G	L	A	D	X	R	T	I	R
W	O	C	W	B	A	C	R	M	S	E	P	Y	V	L
B	A	L	S	T	Z	H	H	A	H	G	Q	G	Z	A
B	R	O	L	T	N	D	P	T	T	U	Q	L	S	T
H	D	S	H	M	W	D	O	R	C	E	U	U	S	M
Q	E	I	S	R	J	M	B	R	A	M	R	I	P	I
A	R	N	E	W	S	L	Q	I	V	P	S	L	Q	W
M	J	G	L	X	U	N	X	N	B	S	P	G	J	F
A	W	G	L	N	Z	O	P	G	A	J	I	E	W	Y
M	H	W	E	N	A	L	N	F	I	N	E	F	D	T
T	M	D	R	B	H	U	Y	E	B	Q	C	D	R	U

Answers

3 Spelling rules

Page 39

1 kittens, cows, desks, casks, branches, foxes, pens, masses, quizzes, leashes

2 **a** The books and the glasses were on the tables. **b** There were patches on the dresses.

3 properties, lorries, injuries, lilies, gipsies, rubies, duties, juries, gullies

4 **a** The ladies were on the balconies.
b The copies were in the studies.

Page 40

1 elves, calves, selves, wives, halves, sheaves, safes, gulfs, lives, beliefs

2 **a** The chiefs were at the wharves.
b The reefs could be seen from the roofs.

Quick check

1 ashes, wolves, sounds, porches, patches, skies, fairies, monarchs, jellies, buses, lions, foxes, lasses, gullies, wallabies, dwarves, churches, halves, ditches, theories

2 **a** The butterflies were on the bushes.
b The injuries were caused by the knives.
c His daughters bought the boxes.
d Adults went on the ferries.

Page 41

1 displays, trays, railways, surveys, sprays, buoys, essays, birthdays

2 **a** The jockeys left on their journeys.
b The turkeys roamed into the valleys.

3 flamingos, dominos, tornados, studios, zeros, torpedos

4 **a** The photos were in the studios. **b** The echoes were heard beyond the volcanoes. **c** The mangos were beside the radios.

Page 42

1 staffs, cuffs, bailiffs, mastiffs, bluffs

2 **a** The giraffes were near the edge of the cliffs.

b The sheriffs collected the tariffs at the gate.

Quick check

1 chimneys, echoes, videos, cuffs, storeys, cellos, donkeys

2 patches, lashes, waxes, buzzes, crosses, halves, whiffs

3 monarchs, reefs, safes, chefs, studios, sopranos, reefs

Page 43 How much do you know?

1 **a** The couriers delivered the crystal glasses to the addresses on the boxes.

b The tomatoes, potatoes and avocados were placed in the crisper drawers in the refrigerators.

c In the musical companies the sopranos also played the cellos in the orchestras.

d The giraffes, buffaloes, flamingos and donkeys visited the waterholes regularly.

e The videos about the lives of the wolves were kept in the fireproof safes.

2 **a** echoes, volcanoes **b** mysteries, years **c** monkeys, valleys **d** knives, shelves **e** taxes, deliveries **f** stories, libraries **g** sandwiches, studios **h** chimneys, wives

Page 44

1 (Sample answers) hungrily, pitiful, victorious, certified, angrily, lazily

2 **a** silliest **b** tidily **c** furious

3 pitying, burying, certifying, occupying, tarrying, allaying

4 **a** enjoyed **b** conveyed **c** buyers

Page 45

1 (Sample answers) quotable, measurable, conical, coming, grazier, insinuation

2 **a** likable **b** graduation **c** glazier

3 useful, movement, sameness, placement, shameless, shapeless

4 **a** safety **b** tuneful **c** ageless

Page 46 How much do you know?

1 **a** 9 **b** 11 **c** 10 **d** 7

Answers

2 **a** No, nervous, 10 **b** No, carrying, 8 **c** Yes, 10 **d** Yes, 7 **e** No, princely, 11 **f** No, pitiless, 7

3 **a** paid **b** agreeable **c** changeable **d** wisdom **e** wholly

4 **a** graceful **b** laziness **c** finest **d** qualified **e** scampering **f** misused

Page 47

1 (Sample answers) beggar, ridding, thinner, bigger, tripping, letter

2 **a** dammed **b** drugged **c** wedding

3 (Sample answers) admitted, regretted, compelled, cruelly

4 **a** preferred **b** allotted **c** beginning

Page 48

1 (Sample answers) leaping, leaner, toiling, teeming, drooped, landed

2 **a** linkage **b** mildest **c** painter

3 (Sample answers) bordered, benefited, murmuring, wandering

4 **a** shouldered **b** whispered **c** wandering

Page 49 How much do you know?

1 **a** 12 **b** 16 **c** 13 **d** 15

2 **a** No, predictable, 16 **b** No, projected, 16 **c** No, leaping, 15 **d** Yes, 14 **e** No, setting, 12 **f** Yes, 12

3 **a** woollen **b** kidnapped **c** worshipped **d** handicapped

4 **a** concealed **b** beginning **c** barred **d** grinned **e** rejected **f** repelled

Page 50

1 handful, harmful, faithful, wonderful, spoonful, cheerful

2 dislocate, displace

3 miscount, misjudge

4 advantageous, manageable, peaceable, serviceable

5 meanness, stubbornness, leanness, evenness

Page 51

1 nobly, probably, notably, agreeably

2 really, generally, naturally, joyfully, equally, finally

3 (Sample answers) vigorous, vaporous

Page 52

1 shield, niece, achieve, diesel, perceive

2 **a** licence **b** license **c** prophecy

Page 53 How much do you know?

1 **a** powerful **b** successful **c** thoughtful **d** truthful

2 **a** disapprove **b** miscalculate **c** misdeed **d** disappoint **e** misapply **f** disclose

3 **a** No, suitably, 21 **b** Yes, 20 **c** No, manageable, 19 **d** Yes, 19 **e** No, eventually, 22 **f** No, faithfully, 22

4 **a** honourable **b** practicable **c** seize **d** favourable

5 **a** p **b** g **c** k **d** k **e** g **f** w **g** p **h** t **i** g **j** l **k** w **l** k

6 **a** dying **b** lying **c** tying

Pages 54–55 Review test 3

1 **a** The ferries rounded the buoys at the entrances to the bay.

b The echoes of the sounds could be heard in the valleys.

c His brothers-in-law took the cargoes to the termini.

d Their nephews and their wives learnt the melodies.

2 **a** dairies, families, countries **b** flashes, glasses **c** lives, turkeys, gullies

3 photos, radios, volcanoes, mastiffs, displays, monarchs, men, by-ways, oases, children, oxen, teeth

4 **a** 8 **b** 7 **c** 12 **d** 13 **e** 11 **f** 11 **g** 14 **h** 15

5 **a** No, waltzes, 1 **b** No, lonelier, 7 **c** No, tagging, 12 **d** No, centuries, 2 **e** No, visitor, 16 **f** No, finely, 11 **g** Yes, 4 **h** Yes, 8 **i** No, gulfs, 3 (exception) **j** No, tomatoes, 5

6 **a** laid **b** said **c** living, played **d** knives, scissors **e** heavier, dropped

7 **d** certified **e** shadiest **k** furious **m** lovely **n** bluffs **o** forgotten **p** visitor

Page 56 Puzzle time 3

Crossword 3

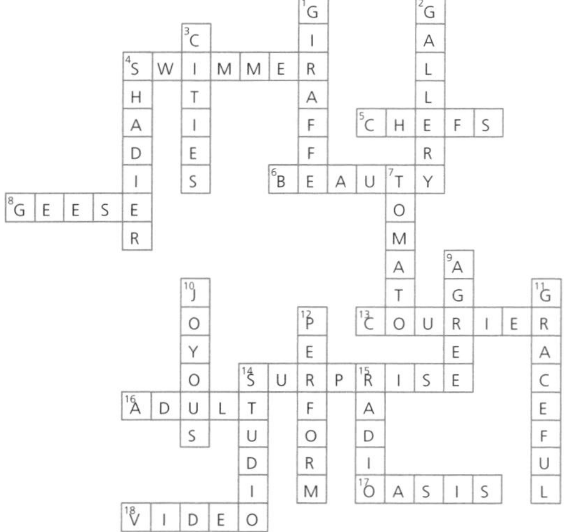

Wordsearch 3

Words: true, deliveries, thieves, display, leap, oases, butterfly, teeth, occupy, wise

4 Word builders: prefixes

Page 57

1 **a** antipathy **b** contraband **c** opponent **d** contrary **e** contravene

2 **a** withstand **b** antiseptic **c** Antarctic **d** contrast **e** obstacle

3 **a** withdrawing **b** antagonism **c** contravention **d** oppression

Page 58

1 **a** overflow **b** superstructure **c** hypothesis **d** underworld **e** suppress

2 **a** overhead **b** supervisor **c** hypothesis **d** underweight **e** submit **f** sustain **g** suspend

3 **a** surveyor **b** suffered **c** supervision

Page 59

1 **a** foretell **b** anticipate **c** precede **d** prologue **e** postscript **f** interfere

2 **a** anticipate **b** antecedent **c** prevent **d** prophecy **e** post mortem **f** intercept

3 **a** preparations **b** anticipation

Page 60

1 **a** decelerate **b** catapult **c** abnormal **d** distract **e** extraneous **f** outlaw **g** parapet

2 **a** parallel **b** outrun **c** extradite **d** dissect **e** catastrophe **f** decrease **g** catalogue

Page 61 How much do you know?

1 withdrew, overgrown, detain, undercut, superhuman, disarray, subside, obstruction, forearm, outrank

2 **a** withstand **b** antagonist **c** opposite **d** contraband

3 (Sample answers) **a** distraction **b** deceleration **c** supervision **d** extraction **e** anticipated **f** overflowed **g** interception **h** prediction

4 **a** para, beside **b** dis, away **c** ab, away **d** out, beyond **e** cata, down **f** de, down

Answers

5 **a** intermix, mix between **b** dislocate, place or locate away **c** avert, turn something away **d** prevent, avoid beforehand

Page 62

1 **a** adjacent **b** attract **c** immigrate **d** perennial **e** dialogue **f** transmit

2 **a** access **b** attach **c** invade **d** translate **e** perspire **f** dialect

3 **a** attractive **b** immigration **c** performance

Page 63

1 **a** exceed **b** uplift **c** midsummer **d** epidemic **e** epicentre **f** educate **g** epilogue

2 **a** expel **b** upright **c** midocean **d** epidemic **e** emigrate

3 **a** education **b** upsetting **c** expelled

Page 64

1 **a** construct **b** commune **c** syndicate **d** symmetry **e** symphony **f** recur

2 **a** conference **b** compare **c** syndicate **d** symbol **e** refer

3 **a** coincidence **b** symmetrical **c** repayment

Page 65

1 **a** uncommon **b** non-event **c** inanimate **d** irresistible **e** circumnavigate **f** circumspect

2 **a** unhealthy **b** invisible **c** irresistible **d** circumvent **e** periscope

3 **a** unlocking **b** impurities **c** circumnavigation

Page 66 How much do you know?

1 transmit, episode, dialect, midstream, convention, expose, insult, inform, midair, persist

2 **a** transfer **b** impose **c** arrangement **d** exceeding

3 (Sample answers) **a** translation **b** perspiration **c** performance **d** emigration **e** transmission **f** construction

4 **a** im, into **b** re, back or again **c** trans, across **d** com, together **e** epi, upon **f** im, into

5 **a** conflict, disagreement with another **b** traverse, travel across **c** adhere, stick to **d** midwinter, middle of the coldest months

Page 67 Review test 4

1 **a** T **b** T **c** T **d** F **e** F **f** T

2 **a** arrest **b** transcription **c** exclaim **d** synod **e** recline **f** illegible

3 (Sample answers) **a** antagonism **b** supervision **c** prevention **d** extradition **e** deceleration **f** oppressor **g** supporter **h** interference **i** abnormality **j** deflection

4 **a** uphill **b** unhappy **c** improbable **d** neither **e** export **f** invalid **g** intolerant **h** unlocked

5 **a** discontent **b** unimproved **c** reinspect **d** unprotected **e** ill-equipped **f** dismember **g** unscientific **h** unappealing **i** disservice **j** reversion **k** unconscious **l** inability **m** uninvited **n** indirect

Page 68 Puzzle time 4

Crossword 4

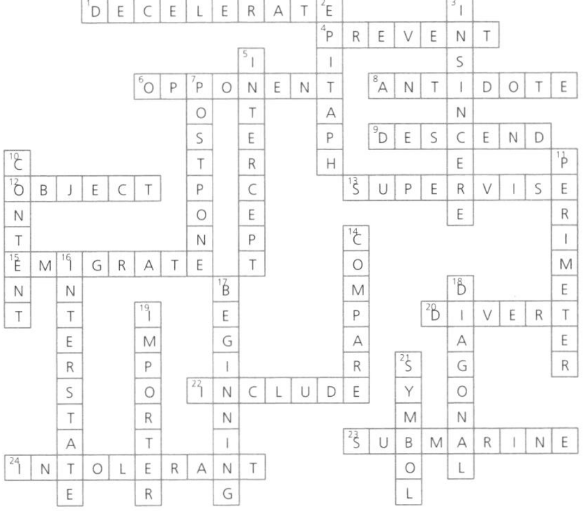

Answers

Wordsearch 4

Words: transfer, eject, submerge, invade, outcast, antonym, arrive, interweave, rejoin, contraband

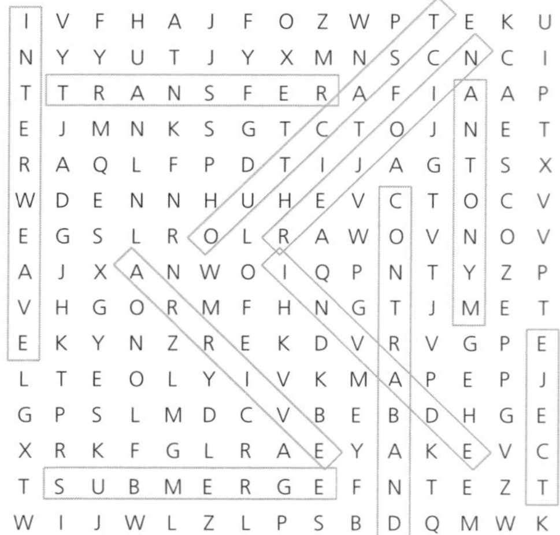

5 Word builders: suffixes

Page 69

1 **a** lawyer **b** florist **c** grazier **d** publican **e** cleric

2 **a** actor **b** tailor **c** botanist **d** trustee **e** electrician

3 **a** governed **b** assisted **c** bought **d** acted

Page 70

1 **a** nourishment **b** multitude **c** humility **d** contentment **e** victory

2 **a** marriage **b** endurance **c** honesty **d** theft **e** brightness

3 (Sample answers) **a** adventurous **b** cowardly **c** obedient **d** victorious **e** abundant **f** weightless

Page 71

1 **a** simplify **b** sympathise **c** brazen **d** simplify **e** publish

2 **a** deepen **b** captivate **c** economise **d** wooden **e** sparkle

3 (Sample answers) **a** abbreviation **b** nourishment **c** baptism **d** polisher **e** economy **f** ripeness

Page 72

1 **a** floweret **b** churlish **c** stormy **d** seaward **e** locket **f** foolish

2 **a** kitten **b** streamlet **c** dirty **d** cloudy **e** gosling

3 **a** foolishly **b** childishness

Page 73 How much do you know?

1 inhabitant, magician, oaten, northward, ringlet, shearer, blindness, strengthen, collector

2 **a** coarseness **b** droplets **c** violinist **d** thicken **e** importance **f** inventor **g** selfish

3 **a** feverish **b** ghostly **c** exercise **d** refugee **e** wealthy **f** jealousy **g** nestling **h** safety

4 **a** -er, one who **b** -y, state of being **c** -ment, state of being **d** -ant, one who **e** -hood, state of being **f** -or, one who **g** -th, state of being **h** -en, made of

5 **a** justice, state of being fair **b** settlement, state of being settled **c** luxury, state of being well off **d** scholar, one who studies **e** spectator, one who looks on

Page 74

1 **a** furious **b** cheerful **c** ceaseless **d** affection **e** thoughtless **f** cautious

2 **a** curious **b** faithful **c** cautious **d** gracious **e** sensation **f** harmless

3 **a** cheerfully **b** harmlessly **c** affectionately **d** occasionally **e** truthfully

Page 75

1 **a** captive **b** rustic **c** curable **d** aviary **e** factory **f** nursery

2 **a** expensive **b** royal **c** audible **d** legible

3 **a** expensively **b** captivity **c** mortally

Page 76 How much do you know?

1 nunnery, powerful, incredible, regular, procession, adventurous, central, rectory, movable, tireless

2 **a** cheerful **b** senseless **c** capital **d** similar

Answers

3 **a** drinkable **b** apiary **c** final **d** pitiful **e** cemetery **f** legible

4 **a** -ful, full of **b** -less, without **c** -ion, the act of **d** -ar, belonging to **e** -ic, belonging to **f** -ible, capable of

5 **a** granary, a place where grain is stored
b popular, belonging to the people
c harmless, without bother or harm
d horrible, capable of causing horror
e contribution, the act of making a donation

Page 77 Review test 5

1 **a** T **b** F **c** T **d** T **e** T **f** F

2 **a** sanctuary **b** singular **c** decimal **d** compassion **e** cautious **f** botanist

3 (Sample answers) **a** builder **b** streamlet **c** collector **d** dictionary **e** cowardice **f** weakness **g** contentment **h** captain **i** mountainous **j** locket **k** rocky **l** electrician

4 cheerful, harmless, pitiful, thoughtless, helpless

5 **a** florist **b** lawyer **c** abundance **d** towards

Page 78 Puzzle time 5

Crossword 5

```
   INCREDIBLE
        A
        N
        G EXPENSE
        E      E   L
       CRITICISE   U
        O A    D C X
        U N    L H U
        S N ENGINEER
      G   E L  N E Y
      O   R E  G R
 N E AVIARY C    F
 O N  E     T  D U
 U J  REGULAR  I L
 R O  N     I  M
 I Y  O   DUCKLING
 SEAWARD    I  N
 H B    ATTRACTION
   L        N  S
MISERY         H
```

Wordsearch 5

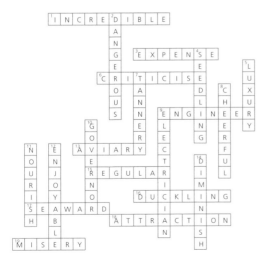

Words: honesty, lunar, visible, ringlet, theft, golden, servant, baptise, cloudy, employee

```
L F T M R Y X Z A A Q W I U O
B O U Q L C R M S D N X L F E
V N V Z N I H E B B O V I G H
G C L O U D Y B I U Q G U G H
Y V W P I G B U A G Y M Q O X
P I S E R V A N T P B N Q L E
N S T H E F T R H L T Q C D M
A I H I F B W I I I U I I E D
D B O A T G B N P E G N S N H
G L N J K N G G C C Y R A E I
Z E E S E M P L O Y E E P R D
J H S R O Y S E R T F J V V R
E D T O J P S T D V W V R N B
J B Y F B S X B U X L J G Z J
S W I M C K X M H C C K T J A
```

6 Word origins: Latin and Greek roots

Page 79

1 **a** inactive **b** auditorium **c** cascade **d** courser **e** cursive **f** decay **g** inaudible **h** agent

2 **a** active **b** inaudible **c** casual **d** current **e** occasional **f** deciduous

3 **a** occur **b** casual **c** active **d** accident **e** decay **f** corridor

4 **a** action, active, actively **b** occurred, occurring **c** accidental, accidentally

Page 80

1 **a** extension **b** credible **c** revise **d** retain **e** extensive **f** creed **g** visible **h** tenant

2 **a** extensively **b** credited **c** revision **d** supervisors **e** entertainment

3 **a** extend **b** discredit **c** visible **d** retain **e** credible **f** entertain

4 **a** tenant **b** retain **c** pretend **d** contain **e** tenacious **f** sustain

5 **a** extend, extensive, extensively
b supervisor, supervisory
c entertainment, entertainer

Answers

Page 81

1 **a** contradict **b** advertisement **c** respiration **d** captor **e** intercept **f** perspire **g** reversible **h** predict

2 **a** acceptable **b** conspirators **c** advertisers **d** indicator **e** convertible

3 **a** dictator **b** contradict **c** predict **d** conversation **e** advertise **f** convert

4 **a** accept **b** capture **c** capable **d** expire **e** contradict **f** indicate

5 **a** convertible, conversion **b** acceptance, acceptable **c** contradiction, contradictory

Page 82

1 **a** manuscript **b** obstacle **c** conspicuous **d** tangent **e** contact **f** suspect **g** stable **h** postscript

2 **a** descriptive **b** tactless **c** suspected **d** contrasting **e** subscription

3 **a** contrast **b** attain **c** contagious **d** tangible **e** spectacular **f** stable

4 **a** conspicuous **b** tact **c** obstinate **d** stationary **e** spectacular **f** spectacle

5 **a** suspect, suspicious, suspiciously **b** attainment, attainable **c** conspicuously, spectacularly

Page 83 How much do you know?

1 **a** T **b** T **c** T **d** T **e** T **f** F **g** F **h** F

2 audience 10, active 4, accident 2, actor 5, agent 7, attain 9, agile 8, advertise 6, accept 1, action 3

3 transaction, inaudible, auditorium, continent, credible, accept, captor, intercept

4 **a** extension, extensive **b** supervisor, supervise **c** dictator, dictatorial **d** converse, conversational **e** description, describe

5 **a** reversible **b** respiratory **c** capturing **d** occasionally

Page 84

1 **a** factory **b** projectile **c** deflect **d** pendulum **e** pendant **f** reflection **g** inject **h** benefactor

2 **a** satisfactorily **b** disinfectant **c** flexibility **d** dependability **e** injection **f** suspension

3 **a** satisfaction **b** dejected **c** objectionable **d** flexible

4 **a** disinfect, disinfects, disinfected, disinfecting, disinfectant, infects, infected, infecting **b** dissatisfy, dissatisfies, dissatisfied, dissatisfying, dissatisfaction, satisfies, satisfied, satisfying, satisfaction satisfactory, satisfactorily

5 sacrificed, sacrificial

Page 85

1 **a** promotion **b** regent **c** opponent **d** conclusion **e** recluse **f** compose **g** director **h** movable

2 **a** promotional **b** regulations **c** composers **d** conclusive **e** mobility **f** disposal

3 **a** irregular **b** positive **c** include **d** promote **e** direct **f** commotion

4 **a** commotion **b** dispose **c** direct **d** oppose **e** compose **f** positive

5 **a** opposition, opposing **b** conclusion, conclusive, conclusively **c** exclude, exclusively

Page 86

1 **a** ancestor **b** expel **c** education **d** construction **e** structure **f** conductor **g** propulsion **h** exceed

2 **a** successfully **b** educational **c** instructions **d** impulsively **e** procedure **f** excessive

3 **a** impulsive **b** expel **c** accessible **d** proceed

4 **a** successful, successfully, succession, unsuccessful, unsuccessfully **b** accession, accessible, accessibly, inaccessible, inaccessibly

5 (Sample answers) procession, instruction

Page 87

1 **a** tractor **b** message **c** cultivation **d** transfusion **e** profusion **f** cultivate **g** transmit **h** extract

Answers

2 **a** attractive **b** emissions **c** transmission **d** agricultural **e** confusion **f** extraction

3 (Sample answers) portraiture, subtraction, contractor, attraction

4 **a** emit **b** attractive **c** dismiss **d** remit **e** colony **f** fusion

5 **a** colonial, colonise **b** attractive, attraction, attractively

Page 88

1 **a** selection **b** repeat **c** fluorescent **d** complete **e** complement **f** confluence **g** repetition **h** legible

2 **a** legendary **b** competitors **c** incompetence **d** fluency **e** influential **f** depletion

3 **a** competently **b** impetuously **c** competitively **d** legibly

4 **a** collect **b** impetuous **c** deplete **d** competent **e** neglect **f** select

5 **a** collect, collective, collectively **b** repetition, repetitive, repetitively

Page 89 How much do you know?

1 **a** T **b** T **c** F **d** T **e** T **f** T **g** F **h** T

2 **a** regularly **b** conductor **c** promotion **d** inflection

3 benefactor, flexible, production, colonial, competent

4 **a** satisfaction, satisfactory **b** reflection, reflect **c** conclusion, conclusive **d** educate, educational **e** repetition, repetitive

5 **a** regulation **b** procession **c** propelled **d** profusion

Page 90

1 **a** animate **b** encourage **c** corps **d** manuscript **e** manufacture **f** incorporate **g** courageous **h** inanimate

2 **a** encouragement **b** courageously **c** cordially **d** management **e** manually **f** managerial

3 **a** courage **b** manage **c** inanimate **d** cordial **e** manual **f** discouragement

4 **a** managed, managing **b** encouraged, encouraging **c** incorporated, incorporating

5 encourage, courageous, courageously

Page 91

1 **a** dentistry **b** biped **c** decapitate **d** biology **e** autobiography **f** captain **g** impede **h** trident

2 **a** pedalled **b** impeding **c** biographical **d** decapitation **e** dental **f** indenture

3 make notches or dents; set back further from margin

4 A biography is a life story told by another person; an autobiography is a self-written life story.

5 capitalise, capitalism

Page 92

1 **a** finale **b** subterranean **c** unite **d** decade **e** decimal **f** unanimous **g** inter **h** confine

2 **a** definition **b** universally **c** decimated **d** refinery **e** uniformity **f** unification

3 confinement, unity, finale

4 **a** finish **b** unite **c** unfinished

5 **a** confined, confining, confinement **b** united, unifying, unification

Page 93

1 **a** civics **b** equator **c** depopulate **d** century **e** centurion **f** civilian **g** equilateral **h** civil

2 **a** civilisation **b** equation **c** populated **d** centuries **e** civilly **f** equable

3 civility, civilisation, equalisation, population

4 equalised, civilised, populated, published

5 **a** equal **b** civil

Page 94

1 **a** metropolitan **b** photocopier **c** geology **d** microbe **e** microphone **f** zoology **g** photograph **h** politics

2 **a** politically **b** photography **c** geological **d** microscopic **e** ornithologist **f** zoologist

Answers

3 a collection of poems
4 instrument for measuring intensity of light
5 very small length of time
6 study of small living things

Page 95

1 **a** phonology **b** geography **c** micrometer **d** synchronise **e** chronological **f** perimeter **g** geometry **h** phoneme

2 **a** phonological **b** geologist **c** barometric **d** synchronisation **e** chronically **f** phonetically

3 machine for playing vinyl recordings

4 picture made by combining several photographs

5 record of events in the order of time

6 meteorological, geometrical

Page 96 How much do you know?

1 **a** T **b** F **c** T **d** F **e** T **f** T

2 geology, political, corporation, encourage, pedestrian, universally

3 **a** encourage, courageous, courageously **b** civility, civilise, civilly **c** equality, equal, equally **d** publicity, publicise, publicly **e** define, definite, definitely

4 **a** fiord **b** porcelain, porous **c** phonetic, phobia **d** mica **e** chromatic, chromium **f** georgette

5 **a** encouragement **b** civility **c** equally **d** microscopic

Page 97 Review test 6

1 **a** T **b** T **c** F **d** T **e** T

2 **a** incredible **b** tenacious **c** perspire **d** postscript

3 **a** objection **b** deflection **c** suspension **d** opposition

4 **a** evident **b** conversation **c** descriptive **d** flexible **e** obstruction

5 continent, credible, impostor, pedestrian

6 **a** inaudible **b** revision **c** regulations

Page 98 Puzzle time 6

Crossword 6

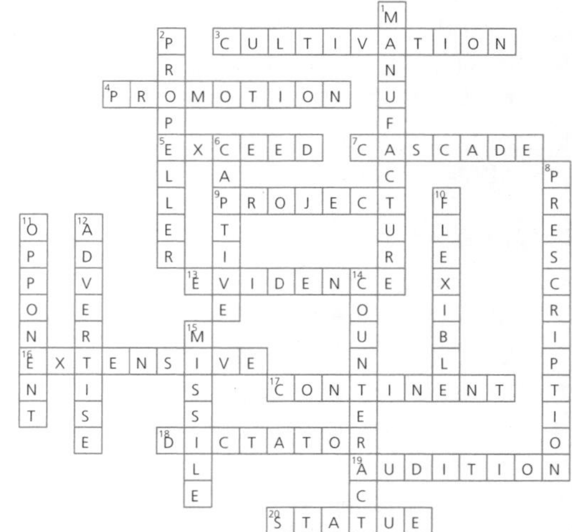

Wordsearch 6

Words: expel, successful, occasional, refusal, contact, recluse, fluid, cursory, capable, factor

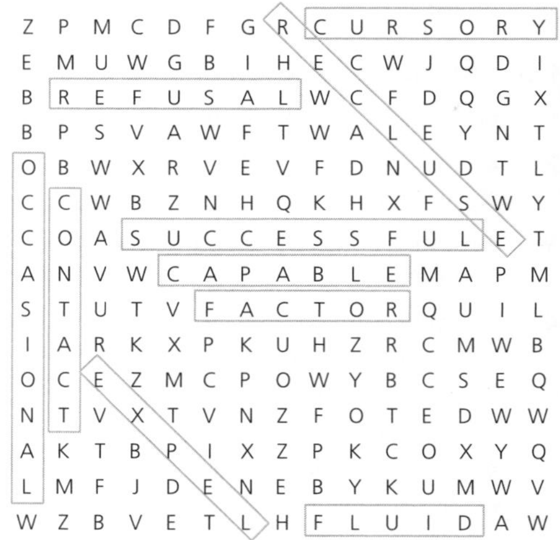